WRITING AND TALKING
ABOUT CULTURE

WRITING AND TALKING
ABOUT CULTURE

John Astley

This monograph is published by EDSERS 2023
www.edsers.co.uk

ISBN 978-1-916838-39-0

Designed and typeset by Copyrite, Exmouth
Printed by Biddles Books, King's Lynn

Other recent books by John Astley

Liberation & Domestication: Young People,
Youth Policy and Cultural Creativity. 2005

Culture and Creativity: The Beatles and Other Essays. 2006

Professionalism and Practice: Culture, Values and Service. 2006

Why Don't We Do It In The Road? The Beatles Phenomenon. 2006

Herbivores & Carnivores: The Struggle for
Democratic Cultural Values in post-War Britain. 2008

Access to Eden: The Rise and Fall of Public Sector Housing Ideals. 2010

Access to Eden: An Essay on Arts & Crafts values, Garden City ideals, and
the 'Wheatley' Housing Act of 1924. 2012 (An enlarged second edition)

The Role of Social Science in the Education
of Professional Practitioners. 2018

The Littleham Council Housing Estate. 2020

Sounds Good For Us: An Essay on Music and Everyday Life. 2020

Tragedy in our every lives: the role of popular culture. 2022

Thinking about the Curriculum: An Introduction. 2022

Acknowledgements

Many people helped with this book, but I would particularly mention John O'Leary and Pete Urquhart for their reading and comments, and Rory for the cover and copy editing, Rachel for her many secretarial services.

The book is dedicated to the memory of James Oliver, writer, editor and publisher; a good friend and much missed.

Contents

An Introduction

Over many years I have been both writing and talking about Culture. Quite a lot of my research and writing in the course of my adult life has embraced this practice, from putting together a resource pack on pop music for my school students in 1973, to publishing a monograph, 'Tragedy in our Everyday Lives: The role of popular culture' in 2022. My dual practice as a teacher has, inevitably, meant a lot of talking! Many venues, a wide variety of students, several short courses for adult education enthusiasts, and a multitude of 'one off' talks, including to conference delegates. So, why have I, do I, do it? One reason is that of all the concepts available to me from my 'intellectual toolbox', the concept of values is uppermost in my orientation to the description, explanation and understanding of our everyday lives both individually and collectively. Who and what do we value, high and low? What kind of action taker do these assessments make to our development?

I am also doing all this as a Sociologist. But what does that mean? I have academic qualifications in sociology, and acquired an enormous amount of knowledge and information about other people and their ideas. In short, a lot of facts, to which I bring my values. This is all sociology. I am a practitioner in this discipline, and recognised as such by my peers. I am also an educationist, and have diplomas to prove it. My first doctoral writing was on the often tricky inter-relationship between teaching and doing research, and I can report that there are considerable variations in how all practitioners deal with this issue, self-consciously prioritising one over the other, although usually the teaching focus tends to suffer some neglect. Some of my work in the last twenty years has attempted to address this matter of value and choice. Like many academics I could have stayed in my 'silo' and got on with my scholarship for good or for ill. However, even here I would have been seriously hampered by the increasing marketisation of higher education on the one hand, with a push to encourage students to concentrate on the development of their own 'human capital' in order to make their way in this very market place.

1

There are issues here about identity, but also of giving service to educational clients whoever they might be. I say more about this in my chapter on Adult Education at the end of this essay. (see my 2018 book on this)

For many years from the late 1960s I was teaching and therefore talking most of the time, while also doing some listening. Of course like all teachers I also did a lot of writing; lesson plans, teaching notes based on my task oriented specific reading, thinking and writing, scribbling comments on student essays and so on. I also did this sort of thing for all my extra-institutional talking and writing. As I have done less teaching my writing has increased. The balance has shifted. In academic life there is the convention of writing up, the revision of writing, editing and generally attempting to get it right. Confirmation of 'this what I came to say'.

My 'intellectual toolbox' mentioned above contains ways of looking at what usually might be called sociological problems, or at least the kind of issues that a sociologist might be expected to have some ideas about. The toolbox also includes a wide range of methods of enquiry, of ways that might orient me in to research, and thinking about such research in a way that might be helpful. In my experience too many sociologists become too fixated on the use of one method of enquiry, one way to find out, collect evidence. Their method becomes a fetish even to extent of under-valuing any other evidence from other approaches. The vanity of small differences. In discussing these issues with my students I always emphasised a 'horses for courses' approach; consider what might get the best results in particular circumstances; a survey here, a set of interviews there.

In addition to all this 'approach' stuff I need to mention the actual writing, and writing style. Just like talking, this is in my opinion as a writer, a crucial element. We must try in the process of 'emptying our mind' to avoid 'emptying the room'.

2

Definitions

So, let me start here by offering a definition of Culture; easy to say, but as this essay will demonstrate notoriously difficult to substantiate!

Culture is a process as well as a collection of artefacts; a painting, a piece of music, a novel, a pair of jeans, a tattoo. In turn these, and many other artefacts are endowed with historically and ideologically determined value (even ideas about 'high/the canon, and 'low/popular, art).

Culture should therefore be understood as a 'verb' as well as a 'noun'. Culture is not just a thing, a commodity, fine works of art etcetera, it is also about creativity, about making, including the making of ourselves and others.

So, Culture can be regarded as a field on interaction between;

1. People's social relationships, conventions and customs. This includes a consideration for the centrality of social institutions, e.g. family and schooling.
2. The symbolic forms (e.g. language, or visual, or musical representations) available to them for focusing on, and co-ordinating experience.
3. People's systems of beliefs, values and actions.
4. Their judgements about the good, bad, beautiful and ugly. These personal and collective 'grass roots' judgements can be seen as a 'grounded aesthetic', i.e. not just those handed down in some canon. Indeed, there are invariably arguments around giving of value for any cultural artefact. These are 'sites of struggle' in everyday life and culture. The expression of these fought over and/or negotiated departures from the canon is usually understood as style.
5. And, finally, why are people thinking what they are thinking? What is going on, has been going on in modern society over time, that makes people think what they do, and why they do it? This is part of my task in this essay, but also in my everyday practice as a sociologist

3

of culture, understanding a 'sense' of how people come to place themselves in a totality of everyday life.

Over many hundreds of years, culture, the cultured and civilisation are seen to be the drivers of everyday life. Ideas determine what people think and do. However, this 'idealist' concept has been challenged before and after Marx and Marxism with a 'materialist' conception. People in all their diversity, come first, their very existence, their human labour, physical and intellectual, is what creates ideas. 'Food comes before philosophy' and of course we are looking at a 'chicken and egg' issue here, how could it be otherwise? It is my task to grasp this dynamic process.

As suggested above it is my experience that there are many difficulties associated with the writing process in pursuit of an examination of Culture, for example what can get in the way. Not the least of these issues being our orientation to the task.

'Working on Capital in the British Museum, plagued by creditors and carbuncles, Karl Marx complained not only that nobody had ever written so much about money and had so little of it, but that 'this economic crap' was keeping him from writing his big book on Balzac. His work is studded with allusions to Homer, Sophocles, Rabelais, Shakespeare, Cervantes, Goethe and scores of other authors…As a young man Marx wanted to be a poet, not a political theorist…' (Eagleton 2023)

When discussing Marx with my Sociology students I made a point about his writing style, as discussed above for example, but also being journalistic in approach; sarcastic, humorous, ironic and so on. Eagleton himself is one such writer; why use five flatulent words, when two witty and incisive ones would convey the message? But, also alerting them to their current and future writing tasks; focus, priorities and being creative.

I mention these issues of my being a sociologist now, upfront, because it is useful for the reader to know where my starting point is in the study of Culture, and what I can, as a sociologist, bring to that study. For me sociology is a doing thing, and yes I read and write a great deal, perhaps too much, about what other people have already said about issues like Culture. My knowledge base is constantly expanding, and I draw on that knowledge and understanding as I make my way with whatever issue is being considered. At their best Sociologists like 'artists' are proselytisers, people who through their work, ideas and imaginations, seek to offer a real truth of self and society, of life and love. The 'true ideal' of human co-existence. They believe that there is a moral responsibility to enlighten, to educate, to demonstrate the value of virtuous practice, to allay the many false claims that there is no such thing as society. Enlightenment, reason, and social and personal freedom are inseparable. The social contract of common humanity is worthy of constant renewal. There is a totality to life, and culture is ordinary, it belongs to all of us.

There is also here the moral issue of the inter-relation between our professional vocation and seeking to do good in everyday life and practice. Theorists of ethics like Alasdair MacIntyre (1980) and Michael Walzer (1983) have argued that we now live in a society where we cannot assume that people will know how to be virtuous due to the splintering effect on society of selfishness, and uncertainty around shared values. We are forced therefore to 're-invent' a commitment to the golden rule of ethics, namely to do unto other people what we would expect for ourselves. Practitioners like sociologists and 'artists' should find a way, through their practice, research orientations, and educational role, to serve the community in which they live and work. The virtuous practice could according to Walzer being an aspect of a more open and pluralistic society.

As I argue in this essay the relationship between academia, in a series of specialisms like Sociology and English Literature and criticism, is a symbiotic one with 'cultural studies'. Both domains of study feed off each other; and so they should. There is also the political dimension as emphasised by Richard

Johnson;

'Very often Cultural studies…has been formed in a two-sided and highly contradictory relationship between academic knowledges and political aspirations.' (Johnson in Punter p.277)

It is the tensions that Johnson highlights that drives forward the determination to do more work on these explanatory pursuits. One of the goals of those of us enthused by Cultural Studies was to avoid the very commonplace descent into a nihilism that recognises neither core, governing, values, or joining forces with a narrow and isolating academia.

'The tragedy of modernity, as recognised most acutely by Nietzsche, is that modern knowledge can tell us a great deal about how the world works (facts), but nothing whatever about what we should do about it (values).' (Davies 2023)

I mention this in my comments about my own 1960s reflection upon the sociology curriculum on offer, and a widely shared consideration of what to do about it. For me, as I have suggested above, making a wholehearted commitment to education was the way to face up to this dilemma.

I mention all this because a number of the thinkers and writers I am going to discuss, for example Raymond Williams, are, or were not Sociologists in the conventional disciplinary form that I have described. But as I shall discuss below Williams was very concerned about the study of 'knowledge', Epistemology, of which the sociology of knowledge has remained a key area of debate. Likewise, he was regularly writing about 'community', a subject close to the heart of sociology, and an issue around exactly how people derive meaning from their 'lived experience', their cultural life. He was also committed to Socialist ideas about fairness.

Williams also provides me with a valuable checklist and guide to some key issues to be explored. These come from the 'Directions' section i.e. 'where are we going with this', of his 1981 book 'Culture'.

'Cultural sociology...is concerned with the social processes of all cultural production...A sociology of culture must concern itself with the institutions and formations of cultural production...a sociology of culture must also concern itself with the social relations of its specific means of production...a sociology must further and most obviously concern itself with specific art forms...' (Williams 1981 p.30/31)

He also emphasises a key issue for me of how cultures and culture groups reproduce themselves over time, and the reasons for that happening, defensiveness and so on. Finally, from his programme is to ask questions about cultural organisations and organising. I spend some time on this issue in my section on the Media. On the specific 'artistic forms' issue, I have spent a good deal of time doing this via my books on 'The Beatles', on Music and everyday life, on Drama, on Architecture and the Arts & Crafts movement, and so on. Researching and writing (and often talking) about these specific examples has obviously developed my more general and contextual work

Structure, Culture and Agency

This also raises a key theoretical issue and debate about how we become the people we are, what are the key influences on our development as a person, a social being? Put simply there is a Structuralism that emphasises the way structural, 'institutionalised' factors, like family, locality/community, social class, schooling and work, are the ones that dominate our personal and social development. Sociologists usually call this 'socialisation and social control', learning our allotted roles and attendant rules. All it bit 'top down', as if we are a 'blank sheet of paper' upon which our everyday life is written. Even the views of F.R.Leavis with his traditional organic cultures in questions of taste is a top-down view. (For more on this see Eagleton 2016 p.146/7) The Culturalism explanation argues that the culture group that we belong to has more influence in how we understand the world and make sense of ourselves. More home grown and culturally interactive, with some agency (wiggle room) for us at the outset.

Structuralism 'sees' Culturalism as too subjective and vague, while Culturalism suggests that structuralism is too deterministic, and in its pursuit of objectivity omits the input of the individual as a thinking, interpretive, and action taking person. It will become clear to the reader that what follows in this essay is much closer to Culturalism. These debates are close to the discussions amongst Marxist scholars, and taken up by Williams in a famous essay from 1973 on 'Base and Superstructure', where he argued that our everyday cultural lives did have a semi-autonomy from the economic and political 'base' of society, the structuralism bit, which he sees as too deterministic. We also have to contend with the idea proposed by many theorists that a tension exists between 'structure' as discussed here and 'action'. The latter concept emphasises that despite many similarities between us all in society, we are all individuals, our unique selves. This is complex and messy, but emphasises the many ways in which we are all thinking and action taking beings making choices. How much agency we have in life will depend a great deal on the structure stuff as well as our capacity as individuals to do things. Many issues raised in this essay touch on this debate.

There is also the issue therefore of studying culture in the various ways I discuss below, and Cultural Studies (CS) which has over recent decades become an academic discipline for students to study, and an industry of book writing, publishing, conferences and so on. The establishment of a canon, a mountain of writings, theories, an enlightening body of knowledge, but also somewhat sanitised to meet the requirements and rules of academia. But, despite all this structure the boundaries of CS are very porous and vague. I would argue that 'cultural studies' is an approach, a way of looking, even seeing issues with the contemporary world that require our thought and attention.

Before continuing to discuss the history, nature and role of Cultural Studies I thought it might be interesting for the reader to see a brief extract from my 2020 book 'Sounds good for us: An essay on music and everyday life.' There are obviously some overlaps and repetitions with this new essay, but I hope this addition considers the issues of cultural studies from a slightly different perspective.

The Role of Cultural Studies

Explaining and understanding cultural phenomena like the creative arts and the artist, requires us to consider at least two levels of engagement. What we can see, hear, experience in the everyday moment as one level of understanding, needs to be supplemented by a 'looking back' to the historical developments that could create the conditions for that phenomenon to occur. This approach was central to the development of Cultural Studies at The Centre for Contemporary Cultural Studies (CCCS) at Birmingham in the work of Hoggart, Hall and their colleagues in the 1970s.

I will be saying more about these approaches to explaining and understanding cultural creativity and development throughout this essay, but to summarise my methodology, the way I think about music, as a sociologist taking a social constructionist view. Society makes music while music makes society; this is a two-way street of affects and effects. I will also be looking at the role of particular cultural groups in the production and consumption of 'their' music. And, as already touched on, there is the perspective of evaluating specific music as art objects that make a contribution to our everyday lives. I mentioned 'looking back' above, which begs the question of where am I looking, what is my focus, whose past comes in to my purview, and what am I not seeing? It may be that what I wish to consider has no 'history' for me to look back to, or at least not as easily available to me as other histories? If we look to the domain of literature we can see an increasing vogue for 'historical fiction', an imaginative way to present the past which deliberately, even boldly filling in some narrative 'gaps'. This goes beyond what we know Historically.

Malcolm Gaskill in a review of C.J.Sansom's historical novel 'Tombland', raises just this issue with reference to another such example, 'Wolf Hall';

'...Wolf Hall refreshes the parts of the past academic history cannot reach. Mantel has zeroed in on gaps in the archival record, the shallows and silences of the past, and exercises there her...historical vision, extrapolating and triangulating from well-documented lives and incidents. Good fiction depends on the truth of human experience.' (Gaskill 2020)

Gaskill adds that Christopher Sansom is equally as good at this.

This happens in music as well; not just in literary accounts of musicians say, but composers 'completing' a piece of unfinished music based on what the original composer left. The completion of Elgar's Third Symphony by Anthony Payne comes to mind. The 'recording' of cultural artefacts by social and cultural historians often has something of the amanuensis about it. So while it is obvious that any culture has a history, how do we, now, come to know about it, even before we consider an interpretation?

But for now some more background to the role of 'cultural studies' might help the reader.

We should not allow ourselves to be compromised in a focus on 'cultural studies', as distinct from the sociological study of 'culture'. The great value of what in the 1960s came to be known as Cultural Studies was that its proponents asked some difficult, but essential questions about the development and nature of post 1945 industrial, capitalist and increasingly consumerist societies. This fundamental concern with asking questions which most social science was not asking, was linked to a post 1945 shift in social relations and an increasing call for democracy, and a cultural democracy at that. Individual freedom (agency), and a real time change in the organisation of everyday life and attitudes was anticipated. The so called generation gap epitomised this.

Cultural Studies in the seminal work of Raymond Williams and others looked at the oppositional literary tradition of Leavis, and of orthodox Marxism in the late Twentieth century, and found them both inadequate approaches to address the issues around understanding what led people of all classes to think, and to do what they did. Cultural Studies sought to put the detailed study of everyday ways of life, focusing on creativity, and the production of cultural products at the centre of any enquiry. One question that always featured in discussions was what social conditions, and socio-economic relations need to exist to allow this or that cultural phenomenon to happen. Cultural Studies was first and foremost an approach, both theoretically and in the research methods used to question the intellectual journey that our cultural lives were embarked upon. Cultural Studies also had to address the deep pessimism of intellectual work done in the 1930s and 1940s on the arts, and on music in particular. The focus by Adorno (already cited) and some of his Frankfurt School colleagues on the rise of mass society and culture. They argued that the advent of a more liberal democratic and welfarist society emphasised the loss of hope that the arts, as one aspect of greater democracy, might liberate people through a raised political and aesthetic consciousness. The rise of mass culture it was argued proved that consumerist capitalism had triumphed in the Twentieth century, and the hope for greater democracy and freedom wasted. Cultural Studies work challenged this pessimism and sought to demonstrate how oppositional culture was in fact alive and well, as was the creatively raised awareness of utopian alternatives via practical, aesthetically grounded, everyday cultural actions. However, the pessimism was strong, even in the 1960s when the prospect of freedom and liberation seemed high.

A further paradox along these lines is raised in D.J. Taylor's novel 'Rock and Roll is Life' (2018), where his protagonist Nick Du Pont becomes a 1960s pop music industry publicist after a brief spell in the U.S.A. working in the same roll in American politics. This raises the whole spectre of the 'spin doctor', a person in a role that sets out to promote and dissemble in equal measure. Adorno's response to this would be to say 'I told you so!'

11

Critical Theorists via 'cultural studies' have for many years now challenged these dominating myths of the gradual progress to a more open and culturally civilised society, and see this vanity of small differences for what it is, a crude device by elites to hold on to their power and privileges. A process of reinforcing their sense of entitlement, adjusting to challenges, and using consumerism to dupe people in to a belief that democracy is on the way; to the shopping mall.

At this point it is also worth reminding ourselves of some fundamental ideas associated with the concept of culture that I am using throughout this essay. The concept refers to the lived experience of people; it is the creative, created, worked on over time product of our existence, and our reflection upon that existence for good or for ill. There is a dialectic at work here; thesis, anti-thesis and synthesis.

My methodology for the study of cultures is to see the inter-relation between the social structures of which we are all a part (family, community, school, work and so on), our particular culture group(s), and our unique biography. The 'balance' between these changes in time and space. This forms a key set of contexts in to which I have set the question; so, what role does music play here for us all?

As already suggested a key aspect of the human condition is that we are reflexive beings, capable of thinking about our situation with a view to action taking. This approach to lived life and its creative outcomes is now the combined thinking of anthropologists and sociologists, where an emphasis is placed beyond 'just' what culture is, but what culture does. This is especially so in the use of symbols like language, and the arts, to make meanings. One of the key issues addressed in this essay is what meanings are made, by whom, for whom, and in whose interests, and where does our individual and collective use music figure? For example, given the form that meanings have, derived from music or otherwise, can we come to understand the struggles around who has power to make their meanings the ones that matter?

12

However, most people do not regard 'culture' in an abstract way; it is normal everyday life, common sense, routine, taken for granted, the quotidian. We tend to only recognise 'culture' as specific artefacts, a music CD, a painting, a theatrical event, a TV play and so on. These cultural 'products' are consumed, often passively, (little inter-action involved) and traded in the marketplace. These products, known as material culture, are often only engaged by us, the consumers, in a surface relationship, a shallow as distinct from a deep and interrogative engagement.

Although Raymond Williams was right to say that 'culture is ordinary' I would issue a note of warning about the blanket use of the word culture. There is a tendency since the 'cultural turn', when talk of culture as everyday life became widespread, to argue that everything is the outcome of culture, and if that is the case there is not much point in talking about it because clearly it is just like 'Blackpool' running through a stick of rock. Of course many aspects of our 'ways of life' are influenced if not determined by the language we speak, the rituals we attend to, the stuff we believe in, that all has meaning for us, including the and the shared understandings we have with other people, especially people like us. It is because these cultural dimensions of our lives can and do make a difference that is worth discussing them. This is particularly relevant when thinking about the arts in general, and in this case, music.

So given this caveat about its value as a concept; a way of trying to understand our lives; I do wish to say more about culture, and the value of the concept in explaining and understanding our lives. Understanding how music is a soundtrack to our everyday lives. Essentially culture is a process, and a dialectical one at that, as well as a collection of artefacts. Culture can be regarded as the field of inter-action between people's social relationships and conventions, the symbolic forms (including language of course) available to them for focusing on and co-ordinating experience; their systems of belief, value and actions. Within 'cultural studies' this process usually takes us to an understanding of grounded aesthetics, a set of values about creativity,

13

art and life that we inhabit within our culture group(s). As already argued a good part of these cultural processes are dominated by a constant discourse about values; who says what is of value, to whom, and under what conditions. A vocabulary of motives is active here, implicitly or explicitly, that surface and deep issue again. Boundaries exist everywhere related to values, and the inclusive and exclusive forms of these cultures, and cultural products, are guarded by gatekeepers keen to determine who should have access or not.

Having said this, I would also argue that the first post-1945 generation, my generation, weaned on the orange juice and cod-liver oil provided by the social democratic welfare state, allowed us to access to an education way beyond pre-war expectations, and did carry forward those high hopes of the 1950s/1960s. The values of co-operation, caring and sharing that underpinned many of the ideals of those decades did direct many of us in to public sector work; health care, youth, community, social work, and teaching; and also contributed to the considerable growth in the social sciences, particularly at all levels of the education system. For the overwhelming majority of people this was certainly not for a comfy do-gooding sinecure, it was politically and culturally a shot at creating the 'good society', of which we were committed co-operators, advocates and proselytizers. Making such work/vocation choices was a moral decision, which did essentially relate to a firm belief in the importance of the collective over the individual. As Zygmunt Bauman has pointed out this moral choice was allied to a 'politics of principle' as distinct from a 'politics of selfishness'. The development of a post-modern society; i.e. a society that has been increasingly atomised and fragmented which has accelerated possessive individualism over commitments to the communal., created many tensions between ideals and reality. In recent decades our moral choices have increasingly been directed towards understanding ourselves as justifiably selfish individuals entitled to act alone. (Bauman 1995)

I would argue that decisions to increasingly exclude music (and other arts) from the school curriculum, thereby denying access to music for most children, was consistent with the selfish moral choices outlined above.

14

Many writers took up these debates on the nature of s changing society, and one of the most influential texts of this period was 'One Dimensional Man' (1964) by Herbert Marcuse, a leading member of the Frankfurt School of Critical Theorists, who had relocated to California to escape the Nazis. The main thesis of his book is that the world wide industrial working class could no longer be expected to lead (even be interested in) the revolutionary overthrow of capitalism. The working class had been 'softened up' by a degree of democracy, State run welfare systems, relative affluence, more opportunity and some social mobility. They had sold out, and were happier with their possessive individualism, including the torrent of stuff emanating from mass culture, like pop music, and the media in general. Marcuse argued that the hegemonic dominance of the ruling elites, their 'expert' led use of 'soft power', especially in the cultural domain, had rendered the working class politically impotent. The hegemony and cultural power of the ruling elites was, and is just too strong. He therefore argued that those advocating the benefits of revolutionary action should look to young people, especially 'students', and to the peasant and nationalist struggles against imperialism and colonialism across the world.

One Dimensional Man is an odd book in respect of its wider effects on the political left at the time, creating more rather than less optimism for the struggle for socialism. People in the UK and elsewhere listened with interest to Marcuse's analysis, but as I have outlined above, retained a faith in cultural creativity as a way to break this impasse.

So despite this one of the ironies of this optimistic intellectual and artistic development in the 1970s was the gradual institutionalisation of Cultural Studies. This well-meaning but often naïve development of Cultural Studies by enthusiastic adherents was feared by many in 'the academy' because they saw this as an undesirable threat to their power to control the curriculum and educational thinking. The first significant student opposition to these controls of the curriculum and so on, came from Art College students, and later spread throughout HE. But, once Cultural Studies entered higher education, its sails full with the winds of change, the process of institutional narrowing began. (There is a similarity here to my concern about the institutionalisation of the concept of 'reflective practice' amongst 'welfare state' professionals). A good deal of what is argued in this essay about studying everyday life returns to this paradox of the one step forward in offering radical alternatives, to one step back in terms of a misdirection in to a new sanitised orthodoxy and/or academic irrelevance; i.e. the answer to societies problems, its oppressions and repressions, is another journal!

Even if we argue like Williams et al, that cultural life does have a semi-autonomy from the economic life of wage labour; the totality of everyday life is in fact still driven by capitalism's priority of wealth making and capital accumulation over time. The daily dynamics of capitalism, especially so global capitalism, determine these fundamentals by creating structures that are required to feed capitalist money making goals. According to the capitalist's mantra there are no human activities that cannot be turned in to a money making opportunity, and that is certainly true of our everyday relationships with music. The German sociologist Jurgen Habermas, in the 1970s called this the 'colonisation of the lifeworld', and this should remind us of the endless inventiveness of capitalists to seek ways to create wealth and promote private property.

(For more on this see Fraser and Jaeggi 2018)

At this point in my argument the issue of the double hermeneutic needs a brief explanation. The majority of contemporary sociologists, and certainly those interested in 'cultural studies' acknowledge that there is a methodological 'problem' with the interpretation of behaviour, including music related behaviour discussed in this essay. For example, to what do we attribute people's actions, to their thoughts and behaviour? The contexts to a person's life, like their socialisation experience, will have to be taken in to consideration. But, as researchers and analysts we will still be interpreting the actions of this or that person, this and that culture group. In addition to all the facts, all the data that can be accumulated we end up making informed judgements about people and their everyday lives; why this happens and that does not. This is the realm of hermeneutics, i.e. the interpretative explanation and understanding of social action. However, those very subjects of our enquiry have also been doing their interpretation of their lives and loves. For example, their relationship with the arts, and with music. They have been attempting to make sense of it all and coming to some conclusions about what they think, and do, and why. So, as sociologists we are interpreting the interpreters, the double hermeneutic. The technical terms drawn from anthropology are emic, the internal view of life of the subject, the person or cultural group; and etic, the external observers view of the 'insiders' subjectivity. I just thought I needed to make that clear.

I raised this outsider/insider issue in my essay on the 'Beatles Phenomenon' cited earlier in this essay.

If we take a detached, long term view of The Beatles phenomenon, then the tendency is to stand outside of the culture in an attempt to produce analysis. But there are, of course, great dangers here, particularly perhaps in losing sight of the dialectical process by which these historical phenomenon, events, came about. If, however, we adopt a close-up, biographical approach, we encounter difficulties with placing too much emphasis on them, The Beatles, losing sight of the overall passage of time and the overall significance of events – past, present and future.' (Astley 2006 p.188)

Musicians in their adopted and adapted genre, and practice methods, also face these issues. For example, 'folk' music is a musician's reaction to the reaction of 'the people'; their people perhaps, and to events, issues, oppression or repression. Musicians, perhaps particularly singer/songwriters can of course be first direct reactors to such circumstances in everyday life, they are certainly capable of being emotional and empathetic.

The values we hold in general, and about 'the arts' in particular will also be

17

relevant here, and cannot be left out of our discussion. I like William Morris designs, wallpaper, fabrics, and so on. I take pleasure from the colours used, the symbolic representation of natural forms, never attempting to copy nature, but stylistically conveying the organic. But what is also very important for me, for my appreciation of the designs and designing, are the values that are implicit concerning Morris' engagement with art, design and craft working in general. These values are clustered around the demonstration of the creation of, and access to the arts. Through his writing on historical processes, and his political work he took the aesthetics of designing in to the realm of opening up the pleasure of this to the many, not the privileged few.

While on the question of style; touched on earlier; I should add a note on what 'style' means to me as a sociologist and critical theorist. All of the roles we take on, are given and perform, come with rules. These cultural rules seek to form and control our thoughts and deeds, they are an exercise in social control both individually and collectively. However, for complex reasons most of us seek to both adopt and adapt these roles in terms of how they are to be played out over time. We try to find some 'wriggle room' to make these roles more related to us, rather than 'them'. This wriggle room, this achieved space, I call style, our individual and/or collective re-configuration of a social phenomenon like role in our way.

Art of all kinds could be seen as an antidote to alienation, and to 'a life in fragments' (Bauman 1995). And as already suggested I mean by alienation the sense that our own abilities and potential worth as human beings, and our actual labour, are taken over by other entities. The daily travails of everyday life can de-centre a person, and addressing this situation through creative action taking can be therapeutic, especially where there is an opportunity to become our own change agent. This can of course be both for the individual as for the culture group

One of the really valuable attributes of The Centre for Contemporary Cultural Studies (CCCS) created by Richard Hoggart and his colleagues in 1964, and based at Birmingham University Department of English, where Hoggart was head of department, was an openness to 'new' ideas and methodologies. The leadership of CCCS was passed to Stuart Hall, Hoggart's deputy, in 1967, who sought with colleagues leadership of CCCS was passed to Stuart Hall in 1967 who sought with colleagues to view the whole complexity of society, to make sense of social change in, and of culture, in its totality.

'to make intelligible the real movement of culture as it is registered in social life, in group and class relations, in politics and institutions, in values and ideas.'

Of course, as I have suggested here, CS now has an enormous history, an archive that any aspiring student of the study of culture has to engage with; the designers of, and teachers of, CS courses have to make selections from the greatest hits to present as an authentic introduction. Good luck with that. A paradox of the work of CCCS was both a focus on diversity and challenges to orthodoxy, was also a focus on 'Cultural Studies' that often led to the problems mentioned here, and as discussed in this essay, whether this institutionalisation has 'watered' down the original Critical Theory and socialist edge? It could be argued that this re-focusing of CS is an acceptable compromise in order to spread the message; I am not so sure, but hindsight is a wonderful thing! But, one of the important issues here is that over the course of the last forty years many (mainly young) people have engaged with CS in one form or another. What has been the lasting effect of that experience? Have that generation been imbued by CS, had their values oriented towards critique of the status quo and so on? There is a piece of ethnographic doctoral research in there for someone.

I have always believed our early lives gives us, even imposes on us, a culture, a way of life, a set of values, that contributes to both an understanding of who we are, our identity, but also who we want to be. I also wish to assert that we are all creative agents of our own, and often other people's culture. We are all born in to a culture group, and because of our family life, and their connections and values, are most likely to follow suit. This is usually called socialisation, the way we become a social being. Family life, amongst other early influencers, also exercises some social controls over our development. Why wouldn't our families, and school teachers, want us to be like them? But, these twin forces can, and often do, create tensions.

As a Sociologist, especially one so focused on the study of 'culture', it is inevitable that using theory plays an important role in my daily practice. And, as I have briefly outlined, there are plenty of theories in use offering explanations of Culture, and these theories are continually debated and used actively in research. This is by definition a very eclectic field of study, and in this essay I shall attempt to show how defining and researching Culture is a doing thing, theorising and researching, as well as knowing. These processes are also about discourses, who says what to whom, and why, in what contexts?

The Role of Theory

Before developing some answers to these questions I should pause to offer what I regularly did for my students, a health warning on 'Theory'.

'To be advised that one should go and read some theory or, worse still, do some theory can be an intimidating experience.' (Macey 2000 p.1)

Indeed, the very mention of the 'T' word is enough to send many people scurrying for cover. Ironically both too much and too little has been made of theory. Too much because theory, theorists and theorising has been mythologised in to an activity reserved for certain kinds of people. To emulate Raymond Williams in his famous statement that 'culture is ordinary', I would offer 'theory and theorising is ordinary'. We all do it all the time. We all have theories about society, people, certain kinds of gender, behaviour, the future, the past and so on. We inherit, and often reproduce such theories, without much additional thinking and consideration. And, in Sociology as elsewhere. these theorists and the theory they offer, is from dead white and middle class males! These are usually 'theories in use', implicit rather than explicit, usually unchallenged; we know who and what we like and do not like. We often espouse theories to fit time and place, but fail to actually behave in such a way. As I discuss in this this essay professionalisation has not helped with this problem with 'the sacred texts', 'chapter and verse'. The obsession with certain kinds of sanctified theory which forms the basis of an agreed body of knowledge has often caused barriers to thinking about alternatives. For example, one of the interesting aspects of the development of Cultural Studies has been the exposure to ideas and bodies of theory from 'those damn continental European theorists with their fancy ideas!' We all need to acknowledge the origins of our theoretical base, especially if the culture we inhabit and seek to maintain is conservative and unimaginative. What Perry Anderson once called 'cultivated backwardness' and anti-intellectualism.

One of my Sociological heroes, the American, Charles Wright Mills gives us a good start in questioning the key contexts to our everyday theoretical and cultural lives;

'The sociological imagination enables its possessor to understand the larger historical scene in terms of its meaning for the inner life and the external career of a variety of individuals. It enables him to take into account how individuals, in the welter of their daily experience, often become falsely conscious of their social positions. Within this welter, the framework of modern society is sought, and within that framework the psychologies of a variety of men and women are formulated. By such means the personal uneasiness of individuals is focused upon explicit troubles and indifferences of publics is transformed into involvement with public issues.' (Mills 1959 p.5)

Mills taught me to locate myself within the complexity of the inter-action between society, cultures and self. He also focused on the absolute necessity to grasp the human condition in an imaginative way. As Sociologists our key method of unravelling the messy nature of everyday life is to take an imaginative leap to an empathy that allows us to understand and connect. One of the real difficulties of writing about Culture, is that it is writing; not talking, painting, playing music, dancing and so on. The experience of life in all its messy and complex sensuous self, requires technique to get down on paper, to transcribe the one to the other. This fundamental theme of the imaginative grasp will be considered in this essay, starting with a more specific account of culture. He also alerted me to the importance of the concept of role as being essential to understanding everyday life. Mills argued that role had two major aspects to it, one public, the other private. Many of the roles we have, or take on, are due to our time and place within the social and cultural fabric of life; son, sibling, parent, partner, student, friend, worker and so on. There are always a set of social and cultural, and historical, 'rules' including expectations, that come with roles, and these have a significant bearing on how we inherit, interpret, adopt and adapt to this role taking and making. However, we also need to assess the manner in which we deal with the private

22

and public dimensions of these processes. How much of our private selves do we commit to any role we have? Do we, can we, develop the skills necessary to navigate our commitment to role taking and performance, to put on 'the public face' that is expected, required, for our own sake and that of others? In our daily social interactions, where we constantly play our many and varied roles, which part of us is doing the 'face' work, the talking, the action taking? We also have to address the issue of whether we are 'one self', or in fact multiple selves? We have to choose on needs and protocol basis which of our selves has to be brought in to play at any time. This may rely on intuition, and/or on experience. Some people are better at this than others. Self and society tensions are there, and the demands of our everyday cultural life are of the uppermost importance in all these issues about our identity; who we think we are, and who other people think we are. And, of course there are echoes here of the Base and Superstructure debate I discussed earlier.

As Terry Eagleton has said of Raymond Williams' work;

'It brought together two senses of the word "culture" by showing that culture in the sense of the artistic and intellectual life of a society manifested certain qualities of life, qualities of being, qualities of relationship and creativity, which needed to be generalised throughout social life as a whole. And the hinge or bridge between these two ideas of culture, the way the first would be transformed into the second, was by politics.' (Eagleton 2008 p.15)

There is also the 'making' of a culture, or sub-culture, that as I discuss elsewhere, emphasises the creative, and 'Magpie' nature of this do-it-yourself process. This is usually referred to as 'bricolage', where we see myth making, the accumulation of self-referential story-telling, reinforcing identity, a sense self and being part of a knowable community. Almost a collective 'auto-biography' of who we are, and survived. As I shall discuss in more detail later, these actions have often resulted in an 'autobiographical fiction.'

What is also essential to say is that 'nature', especially perhaps the flora and fauna of our everyday lives, must be considered as a key aspect of Culture in both standard respects, ideas and use. In contemporary life the discourses around climate change, the use and abuse of the environment, the role of agriculture in the management of the 'countryside', the value of engagement with 'the land and the sea', and so on, has an enormous place in our everyday lives. We talk and write about it, it is very political, creates great emotions in people, and takes up a lot of TV! (See Punter page 71 0f his cited text for more on this) Over many centuries we have defined and redefined 'nature' usually not out of veneration but in order to tame and control it. Over such a time scale it is clear that everyday human life was inextricably a part of nature, not at some objectified and subjectified distance, another 'other' in our lives. For many people the value of nature is primarily a spiritual one, religious or otherwise. The jadedness that can be all too apparent in our age (as in the past) can be mediated by engagement with nature, returning to an often mythologised innocence seems very attractive for some. The gap between 'the real' nature and the imagined one is always with us, and redolent in our objective and subjective cultures, not the least of which issues being the changing division of labour, especially between mental and manual labour and the whole debate around where our ideas, our consciousness comes from? At the very least let's remind ourselves where the word 'culture' come from! The significant social and economic changes, like the 'industrial revolution' of the late nineteenth century, with extensive migration of people from the country to the growing cities to populate the factories created a need in many people to set aside their alienation by spending time in the countryside, walking, cycling and so on.

Raymond Williams has often set the tone of our inter-relationship with nature, ideas and hands-on, for example in his 1973 autobiographical book 'The Country and the City' where amongst much else his considers changing attitudes to 'the country' in its dynamic relation with the burgeoning city. There is here, over time, a growing and now formalised, and institutionalised inter-dependence of the country with the city now known at an abstract level and/or a skewed focus for example of 'tourism'. These human and real world particulars, including the conditions of both production and consumption. The media, usually allied to advertising, has created a series of images and ideas that in a symbolic way comes to a taken for granted version of both country and city, a 'picture-postcard' representation of place where the labour of those serving both, are left out, ignored. The National Trust, along with much of the Heritage industry, were, and still are some of the worst culprits in this regard.

In considering the development of English Literature Williams spent a good deal of time discussing the literary accounts of nature in novella and poems. His fiction also addresses the complexity and paradox of country life and landscape in his early novel 'Border Country' (1960).

So, if it important to Williams, we should take note, and connect up our general thinking about our cultural lives, and the planet on which we live, the meanings we have made and un-made over many years.

Popular and Pop

Throughout this essay there will be discussed both 'popular culture' and 'pop culture'. This apparent bifurcation of culture has occupied many people since the 1950s, and became a particular area of confusion and consternation in the 1960s. George Melly, for me the author of the best introductory book on these issues suggests;

'Both popular and pop culture are of working-class origin, and both arose out of a given situation both social and economic. The principal difference is that popular culture was unconscious, or perhaps unselfconscious would be more exact, whereas pop culture came about as the result of a deliberate search for objects, clothes, music, heroes and attitudes which could help to define a stance...Popular culture, although naturally subject to regional differences and increasingly corrupted by the early mass media and the spread of gentility, had grown slowly...' (Melly 1972 p.3/4)

These key issues will be examined a good deal over the course of this essay, and from Hoggart in the 1950s onwards, have led to both the development of 'Cultural Studies', and heated debates on the main cultural drivers in our everyday lives, and, the best ways to explain all this. Not the least of questions here is how did 'pop culture', particularly the music, become so popular; a key issue that I addressed in my book on the Beatles Phenomenon. Can this really be attributed to the cultural power of the owners and producers, and the 'sheep like' behaviour of consumers? Are people's choices due to their lack of viable alternatives, lack of imagination, or plain intellectual laziness? It was once common place for a wide variety of commentators on popular culture (certainly on the conservative right) to talk of Mass Culture; the culture of 'the masses', those very same 'sheep'. This perspective was often tied to the concept of the Mass Media of Communications, especially TV and Pop Music, and once again posed the view that people were increasingly homogeneous in their tastes and always persuaded by the owners and

26

controllers of these cultural organisations, for good or for ill. This issue will regularly be considered in this essay, part of the task of Cultural Studies has been to challenge this simplistic idea.

One thing is quite clear in that many researchers, writers and talkers, have drifted away from these core issues around 'Culture' to concentrate their attention on the 'objects' of cultural production, the flotsam and jetsam of an increasingly consumer led cultural life. People are 'allowed' to embrace their frivolity, and 'thoughtlessness'. Looking at these issues we are moving in to discussions about 'reification' which mean the way social relations between people, and people to objects, becomes 'thing-like'; the human and humane dimension of all this is sucked out of relations. The Nazis, on their way to an 'industrial solution' of what to do with the Jews, they turned them in to 'things'. A typical approach of British colonialists, especially so in Africa, was to see people as sub-human, making any moral dilemmas easy to deal with. Constant cultural reinforcement for a set of values and a psychology that that did not need much encouragement. The hubris of believing their own propaganda.

Objectification, non-human-ness in everyday life, dominates this whole period of cultural life and is full of paradoxes and miss-interpretations. Popular means 'the people', but we all know that this 'people' are not a homogeneous group. But, it would seem that if we simply do some bean counting very many people do watch the same TV, listen to the same music, and wear the same cloths etcetera. Their tastes like their values do seem very similar, very uniform. Recent evidence would however suggest that increasing numbers of consumers have very diverse usage behaviour within choosing to behave in very similar ways. There is always some divergence from what seems to be the social and cultural norm. These differences do represent what is usually referred to as 'signifying practices' i.e. individual and/or groups 'showing' us something different, which for them, and for observers of these behaviours, say something about their otherness.

27

Take for example the impact of 'pop' artists like Richard Hamilton with his 1956 collage celebrating the wonders of the acquisitive society and consumer capitalism at exactly the time when Hoggart was highlighting the dangers of just that, and I regularly comment on the 'conservative' nature of much so called popular culture; equally as much as the consistent conservative form of most so called 'high culture'. So, what are we to make of people's choices of entertainment and so on? Like so much art, certainly then, as now the use and role of irony gets in the way.

Hamilton, like many of his peers, was anti-capitalist, but did everyone witnessing, aspiring to, and living this, get it? As usual there is art, and then there are ideas about art! Modernism, like all 'isms' is about ideas, which reinforces the debates about the meaning of art, and meaning in art.

There is also therefore the on-going issue as highlighted by Melly, of the motivations behind 'pop' culture, which like the motivations of an avant-garde in the arts, is to challenge the status quo. And, a status que that at some time had been progressive, acknowledged as in the vanguard of change. Established cultural tropes, and the very artefacts themselves, usually well and truly commodified, become a conservative cultural influence. For example, people (often men) for whom 1970s Rock Music epitomises the values of their youth, and still do, their musical taste frozen in time; nostalgic, safe, and self-referential. This phenomenon exists across all culture, and as already argued often forms a key aspect of 'popular culture', tried and trusted, conventional, utilitarian.

There are also here more general concerns about the everyday situation that most people, working class or otherwise are outsiders to 'art' as perceived in its more formal kind. Of course many, even most, art products are available to all people on a daily basis, but are not engaged with because of cultural as well as economic or geographical reasons. At the entrance to galleries, or box offices for 'high art' products like opera or Shakespeare, there are no signs posted to deliberately exclude people, but of course these are not needed as most people exclude themselves on the basis of taste and so on. There have been endless amounts of hand-wringing by the well-meaning people who operate art galleries for example to reach out to encourage people to step over the threshold. 'Come and look at what the artist has made'. Curators of galleries etcetera have now realised that this outreach work is a fruitless task, and have turned instead to making their resources available to people to demonstrate their own sectional interests. There is a deep irony in this debate because of course most galleries etcetera receive public, i.e. taxpayer's money to do what they do. And, this is supposed to be good for us, a part of the civilising process.

Most people know from their own life experience and everyday cultural lives that this is not for them. What is of interest is that many other cultural producers do not seek to 'show' their work in these ways in the general course of their life and work. Architects and designers tend not to invite people to see their products in this way, their work is shown in a more generally commonplace way. Most farmers do not have a sign at the farm gate inviting people to come in and look at their latest production. Of course all such groups of 'producers' work is seen, for example at agricultural shows, and new housing developments, but not often in the rarefied atmosphere of much 'art'.

I will raise these core, and problematic issues again in my chapter looking at 'The Media', and the chapter on 'Hegemony'. These are simply early skirmishes!

To add to the discussion so far on forms of culture, including their conservative and radical aspects, I would say that for me Williams sought to remind us; especially in moments of frustration and disappointment; that the outcomes of creativity of an artistic, intellectual and educational kind, are resources of hope. Feeling and imagination are like bridges, hopefully taking us, individually and collectively, to good places. The very processes of cultural creativity, this action taking, our practice, can expand our horizons, to seek out pastures new. But, is that true of both these cultures?

I should also mention the enduring 'British' sentiment, a nostalgic but positive acknowledgement and pride in being the leaders in the making of 'the industrial revolution', and world leaders in the development of an ironic take on life. The opening ceremony of the 2012 London Olympics proved that beyond any doubt, and the creative energies of Danny Boyle and his co-producers rekindled the triumph of mid twentieth century social democracy and the 'welfare state'. As Dominic Sandbrook has pointed out (2015) Britain may have lost its world leadership role, and Empire, and good riddance to most of that, but had become the home of cultural creativity in all respects; 'The British are coming'!

As I will elaborate in this essay, we should remember that a good deal of our everyday memory is cultural. How exactly we learn, understand, use and pass on 'our culture' will depend on a myriad of factors, not the least of which being our family and locality. Including sport. One important aspect of understanding the creation and use of culture, is that within that culture group, develops over time, so that what we think and do today, has a history. Memory, both individual and collective, plays a significant role. And, as I shall discuss below, who has control of these memories, and how nostalgia is a developed aspect of memory is a key, and often political and ideological issue. There are struggles over the control of memory. We also have to consider the role of imagined communities and invented traditions, which play a considerable role in our personal and even national sense of self. For example, who says what it is to be English? The particular, and pertinent culture may be a contested one today, and will almost certainly have come to us in an 'evolutionary' way as a contested one.

This contestation has often turned to a more radical and even revolutionary response to the status quo. We should also remember that up until the 'industrial- capitalist' era, 'revolution' was used to mean 'a turn back' to better times, to a condition of natural justice, even to the religious code of equality before God.

I will discuss many of these 'struggles' for agency in this essay. But, there is surely a much 'flatter' hierarchy in the way our culture is made, comprised, and lived. There is likely to be a greater expectation of reciprocity in culture groups, an everyday expectation, a social norm, shared values, attached to our inter-actions. Or, as Edward Thompson suggested 'the rituals of mutuality'. We should not overlook the psychological consequences for the person within the different cultural organisations and institutions that they encounter every day, for example the possible differences between home and school. However, and despite all these external factors impinging on any person's life, no one else has lived our particular life; the detail does matter, despite the growing inequalities in society due to private wealth, centralised political power, celebrity status, and obsession with money!

The institutional culture of the school may be at odds with the culture of home life, linguistically and in other ways. The forms that schooling etcetera takes is both ideological i.e. a deliberately formed set of powerful ideas, and has the authority to impose this. The work of Basil Bernstein the leading sociologist of education through the 1960s to his death in 2000, pointed to the consequences of such cultural variations, emphasising what he and Pierre Bourdieu (in France) called 'cultural capital', what it is culturally that families and peer groups instil in to children and young people.

How we live the way we do; and there are good reasons for it, is the way we have become culturally, a 'paid-up' member of that culture group. But there may be consequences of this as we encounter other, and sometimes more powerful, and socially controlling cultures during our socialisation; the process of becoming social beings. As will also be discussed below that our sense of ourselves as members of a culture group is in a shared value for and use of certain 'cultural' goods. These valued objects could be a TV set, forms of music production and consumption, and even mobile phones. For some people valued 'goods' might actually be certificates of educational achievements, blank cheques that can be cashed-in at some time for access to a higher status. Of course this access to status goods can be oppressive, and in terms of our life journey counter-productive.

One other aspect of these phenomena touches on the mores, the customs of everyday life, and the ordinary effects of these deeply cultural values and sentiments, and by definition, sentimentalities. Erin Maglaque writing in the London Review of Books (2023) quotes Kathleen Stewart on these 'ordinary affects';

Which are '…public feelings that begin and end in broad circulation, but they are also that seemingly intimate lives are made of. They give circuits and flows the form of life. They can be experienced as a pleasure or a dragging undertow, as sensibility that snaps into place or a profound disorientation… Their significance lies in the intensities they build and in what thoughts and feelings they make possible.' (Maglaque 2023)

Williams was very aware of these issues, and his idea of 'structures of feeling' discussed in this essay are close by. In addition to all his non-fiction academic writing, of which there is a lot, he developed these ideas through his fiction, a series of novels and plays. The novels, starting with 'Border Country' (1962) as cited, often a fictionalised account of his growing up on the Welsh/English border. This story was followed chronologically, in setting and production by 'Second Generation' (1964) which took the key characters of the previous story to live and work in Oxford, where Williams himself was associated as a university adult education tutor. In the 1980s, while I was living and teaching in Oxford, I devised an adult education course using an in-class reading of this novel as an introduction of Williams' work. Through the medium of his fiction Williams sought to work through, to demonstrate, the interactions that Eagleton highlights.

So, part of the process of Culture is the ongoing debate around relevant and meaningful discourses; who says what to whom and under what conditions. A vocabulary of motives. The grounded aesthetics aspect is also important here in that the means via which people can express, and do their cultural creativity is invariably in a DIY manner; using, adapting and modifying existing technologies, symbol forms and so on. In what ways do we interact with others, near and far? What symbolic characteristics of our life, like language, image, do we take in to these daily inter-actions? In a reference to my citing of Mills earlier, our objective and subjective lives making for communication.

We also have to acknowledge the role of semiology in our thinking. Semiology is the study of signs, and their role in our everyday lives. Take road signs for example, which appear to have a clear role, they have a necessary utility in assisting us to navigate highways and byways. They are universal systems of meaning; 'one way', 'no entry' and so on. But, they are not just an aid, they are instructions, commands even, that have authority. But who says so? Why do we accept these conventions? Take for example the green figure on road crossings to inform pedestrians that they can cross. I have lost count of the number of women, often mothers say, who say to their child that this instruction is from the 'green man'. But why a man? Is this because the symbol on the sign seems to be wearing trousers? Don't women wear trousers? Don't they also have the authority to guide across the road? The theoretical pioneer of this line of thinking and questioning was the French critic Roland Barthes (1915-1980), who with the publication of his book 'Mythologies' in 1957, raised the key issue of the role of myths in our everyday lives; like for example that it is more appropriate for men rather than women to be authority figures. He sought to challenge these assumptions, this apparent acceptance of this status quo within our cultures, and everyday cultural lives.

In relation to the above it is also important to mention Williams' idea about the existence of dominant, residual and emergent cultures. In the section on Hegemony below I will discuss the issue of dominant cultures, related to what I say in this essay about the power of some individuals and groups to dictate taste. Williams argues that even under these apparent circumstances of control, there are in active consideration and everyday use, residual cultures, like 'folk' cultures that are still significant in how people understand their lives and give it meaning. These residual cultures are therefore relevant to the development of 'counter-cultures', oppositional and emergent, that seek to challenge and overturn the dominant. These three 'opposing' cultural forms can be found across the political spectrum, not just on the political 'left'. As we have seen in the last forty years a re-emergence of classic Liberalism has been re-energised and re-branded as Neo-Liberalism, to challenge the post 1945 orthodoxy of the social democracy of the 'post war settlement'; the public domain.

So, according to Williams, Culture is ordinary, and special. Special in the obvious sense that individuals and collectives within culture groups create something out of the ordinary, beyond the quotidian, that exemplifies what their practice is about, perhaps utopian, challenges orthodoxies and represents a significant marker in cultural development. It is also tenacious, hanging on, still creating despite the odds; a little like wild flowers in walls and crevices, which like disparaged and under-valued 'artists' are seen as 'weeds'!

I will return to this issue later. There is also a concern with both the process of Culture, human creativity and so on, and with the organisation and conditions of production of any cultural artefact. What are the conditions of practice that influence the work of any 'artist'? We all make culture, but not necessarily in conditions of our own choosing. This is essential territory for Williams and many others like myself. The objectivity of life, the 'cultural materialism' to which we bring our subjectivity, including our aesthetics, is crucial. Critical Theory is our methodological 'can opener'.

In a more general argument Eagleton touched on a key issue;

'Art can only be studied historically, and yet like all superstructures has its relative autonomy; it is powerless by itself to emancipate men struggling within class-society, and yet, even within the present, can provide powerful images of such emancipation.' (Eagleton in Lifshitz)

34

Those 'powerful images' are part of what art is, can and should be, is vital because it offers an alternative reality. Art is oppositional to 'instrumental reason' (life with the humanity the taken out). As W.H.Auden said to Benjamin Britten in Alan Bennett's play 'It is the habit of art that keeps us alive.'. The good society, the good life, the endurance; ars longa, vita brevis! The possibility of non-alienated labour, William Morris' dream for all humankind. All life should be art, all art life.

I would add that the very existence of 'artists' liberated from the conservative status quo of (dead) white and middle class men, for example the new focus on women and people of colour, is itself a 'powerful image' of such emancipation. Thus recent acquisition of agency is by definition an historical phenomenon, another aspect of alienation challenged by artistic practice by individuals and collectives. Who has agency, and why, is a question we should be asking.

I have already emphasised that theory continues to play a major part in my attempts to understand the lives we all lead, and cultures we make, maintain and change as a consequence of these lives. And, for me theory is very much a verb, theorising/conceptualising, is the key to deciding on what is the most appropriate methodology to progress my enquiry. This always includes examining the body of knowledge available to inform my practice. I have also cited Mills on the inter-relation between society and self, required us to look again at the contexts to our everyday life. Looking again via available theories, can lead to creating our own theoretical pathways to advance our understandings. I shall develop these issues in my pursuit of a better understanding of how my writing and talking on Culture has pushed at theoretical boundaries. As a consequence, therefore, Political Theory is never far away, and for me as a Critical Theorist I want to assert that my use of Critical Theory has helped me to understand the connections between Culture and Politics. Looking at Culture has helped me to understand how our everyday cultural lives are political. Clearly most people do not see every day aspects of their lives, even why and how their cultural life, in all its commonality and specificity, is contextualised by politics.

To sum up these issues I would paraphrase Peter Barry (1995) in that;

1. Politics is pervasive,
2. Language is constitutive, essential to everyday life and living,
3. Truth is provisional, rarely pure and never simple (Oscar Wilde),
4. Meaning is contingent, open to circumstances and interpretation,
5. Human nature is a myth, and idea used to simplify and normalise the complexity of development and knowledge.

These connections have to problematized, to stand out in plain sight, to then be considered worthy of questions being asked, explanations required. We need to ask why we hold the values we do, and to whom do we attribute the origins, maintenance and change of those values? Is this our agency?

This has been how my role has developed, pointing out questions that need to be asked, to be researched, that people did not see as needing to be asked. This realisation of the need to ask questions, to challenge the status quo of thinking beyond the usual, the assumed taken-for-granted known, has been an essential aspect of my writing and talking about Culture. Without wishing to sound like an arrogant know-all, I do want to challenge people to question their own complacency, use their creative imagination to explore; experiential and experimental. For me this has been at the core of my educational role, examining that unexamined life.

So, why have I, like many other people concerned themselves with this Culture stuff? Certainly from my perspective not just as an academic endeavour, abstract and esoteric. Like many people in the great post 1945 tradition of Adult Education, I have felt that there is a need to spread the word, to pass on some truths about just how important our cultural lives are, and why this good news should be shared by all. One of the great truths of 'art' is that it has, does and could challenge the many falsehoods and myths, secrets and lies, that stand between us and the 'good society'. In my experience over many years of practice, and influential encounters, proselytising on behalf of greater enlightenment, and a self-belief driven engagement with the making of culture is an essential way of life. The unexamined life is not worth living, and I am always trying to make sense of myself. These determinations are a part of my conditions of practice, how I do what I do, and why. I shall be saying amore about these issues throughout this essay.

I would add here that Sociologists tend to offer three broad explanations for both existing attitudes and behaviour, and these factors influence on change, personal and collective.

1. There are period effects; the zeitgeist, with all the messy complexities of that.
2. Life cycle effects; ageing does matter, so does role changes, and the implications, consequences, of the myriad roles that we occupy over time, and
3. Cohort effects; the nature of our contemporaries in our time, peer groups, cultural choices, and 'un-choices'.

Add to this the on-going process of interpretation and self-reflection, the reflexive self.

However, before moving on and saying more about Raymond Williams and his contemporaries I need to address the issue of 'postmodernity' and 'postmodernism'. Let me start with Eagleton, a well-known detractor about the validity of both concepts;

'The word postmodernism generally refers to a form of contemporary culture, whereas postmodernity alludes to a specific historical period. Postmodernity is a style of thought which is suspicious of classical notions of truth, reason, identity and objectivity, of the idea of universal progress, or emancipation, of single frameworks, grand narratives or ultimate grounds of explanation.' (Eagleton 1996 p.vii)

The progress of which Eagleton speaks is that which is associated with
Modernity, a coalition of ideas about the growth of industrial, capitalist/
socialist, urbanised, secular and increasingly democratic societies. The
dominant values of the period from at least the end of the eighteenth century
in 'the west' are seen as progressive under the French revolutionary of liberty,
equality and fraternity (cooperative and collaborative society.) To state the
obvious, this is work in progress through a series of revolutionary, and counter
revolutionary upheavals. This is Marx territory of course as his main interest
was what causes revolutionary ruptures and transformations. For Marx these
are historical struggles leading to significant social, economic and cultural
changes. For Marx the issue was what role the newly created industrial
working class would play in these transformations to Modernism, and would
this new state of society be capitalist or socialist? And, as a warning note to all
us scribblers, he has on his gravestone the epigram;

'The philosophers have only interpreted the world in various ways, the
point however is to change it'

So solipsists beware.

The big question here is, are these ideals exhausted, can 'modernity' take
us any further? Have we passed beyond this era in to a radically different
form of social relations and ideas? Sociologists have often referred to this
postmodernist era as 'Post-Fordist', in the sense of beyond manufacturing
(e.g. cars) on a mass production scale. But this is primarily in 'the west',
as a consequence of increasing globalisation of trade, production, and
consumption a good deal of this mass production has moved to Asia.

Post modernity and Postmodernism

'Postmodernism is a style of culture which reflects something of this epochal

38

change, in a depthless, decentred…pluralistic art which blurs the boundaries between "high" and "popular" culture, as well as between art and everyday experience.' (Eagleton 1996 p.vii)

These are issues which are regularly raised in this essay. The point is there are many issues around the nature of culture in the narrow and wider sense that are still being debated, and there are no simple opposites here. However, we do know that postmodernist culture has almost become the cultural norm in how most people think and act in contemporary societies like ours. There is little challenge to the idea that anything goes, that no one has the right now to question the open set of values about the arts. The boundaries between public and private desires have dissolved in to a free-for-all of endless novelty, fashions that are almost entirely about the satisfaction of selfish needs. There is no human activity that cannot be turned in to a money making opportunity. Anything remotely like a history lesson to guide our thoughts and actions has been replaced by the latest guide to the fashionable cultural cul-de-sac.

In 1981, as already cited, Raymond Williams published 'Culture' one of the few serious studies devoted to the complexities of the subject. He had along with many others; like Richard Hoggart (Uses of Literacy), Edward Thompson (The Making of the English Working Class), and Stuart Hall (The Popular Arts; with Paddy Whannel) had set in motion a focus of the making, re-making and significance of Culture, and the necessity to devote time and resources to such a study. Hoggart, and Williams were explicit in the connections they saw in the descriptive value of literature when attempting to capture everyday life, lived in a particular place and time. What has been called a 'thick', in detailed, description, as distinct from a 'thin' and superficial one.

Hoggart and Williams wrote about the distinctive nature of the urban and the rural, and considered the realities and myths about everyday life in these apparently very different environments. What they both showed; Hoggart in 'The Uses of Literacy' and Williams, in particular in 'The Country and the City' was the inherent interconnections between these environments and local cultures, because the condition of life and developments were driven by the needs of capitalists, and capital accumulation whether industrial or agricultural. The process of re-designing agriculture as a profit making and capital accumulation endeavour drove people in to towns to work in factories. This diaspora had profound effects upon indigenous cultures. As Hoggart and Williams both noted, people hold on to what they can of themselves in these enforced transitions, community 'building' on the basis of need and cooperation. And then when not needed in a particular place at a certain time, were disposed of, moved on or abandoned. The costs of agricultural and industrial change still reverberate.

I have recently read 'A Stinging Delight' a memoir by David Storey; artist, novelist and playwright, of whom I was/are, a big fan. Storey was born and brought up in Wakefield in West Yorkshire, the son of a miner, and lived in a period, 1960s/70s when voices from 'the north' were increasingly heard and seen. He was in many ways typical of that generation of 'writers' that epitomised the often awkward journey made by such 'artists' from working class backgrounds and defining cultures, to middle class life and consequent notoriety. 'you can take the boy out of Wakefield, but you can't take Wakefield out of the boy!' Well summed up in Storey's play 'In Celebration' (1969), which highlights that 'half-way-house' situation of many people in that era. I experienced something of that myself as the first child in my kinship group to attend Grammar School in 1955.

In reading Storey's Memoir I was constantly reminded of Richard Hoggart's book 'Uses of Literacy' especially so because of the social and cultural transformations that took place in those twenty years after 1945/50. (Storey was born in 1933, and Hoggart's book published in 1957, drawing on his life either side of the War.)

In reflecting on changes to post-war society and culture, Hoggart argued that;

'…working-class people probably do not feel themselves to be members of a "lower" group as strongly as they did a generation or two ago. Yet those I have in mind still to a considerable extent retain a sense of being in a group of their own…they feel… that they are "working class" in the things they admire and dislike, in "belonging"' (Hoggart p.19)

He made this comment after earlier acknowledging that social and economic changes had taken place, and that in many ways the very distinctive lives of the industrial working classes that were created, 'made', in the 'industrial revolution' from the late eighteenth to the late nineteenth century, was a relatively brief if very intensive period of change and transformation. As I say elsewhere in this essay Hoggart and his contemporaries were responding to these changes and wanted to question the assumptions that the progress to a better life for all, was not without its cultural losses and question marks, against the value of this 'progress'; affluence to what extent, and for what ends? In recent years it has become increasingly evident that the 'jam tomorrow' promises of access to the 'Garden of Eden' have been, exaggerated. Privilege and deprivation and 'underachievement' still make a huge difference to children lives.

As Storey says about the disappointment of the loss of a 'brighter vision', not the least being in the hope of a more equal, fair and democratic life. I wrote about this in my book 'Herbivores and Carnivores'. While cultural critics like Hoggart, Williams, and Thompson were analysing the nature and issues of this time, their concerns were echoed in the artistic practice of Storey, David Mercer, Alan Sillitoe and many others. (see my monograph on 'Tragedy', Astley 2022, for more on this.) We will not see the like of these particular people again, but we can still reflect upon their hopes and frustrations, and crucially the continuation of a 'two tier' society.

My sociological awakening

As a 'trainee' Sociologist I was of course concerned with all these transformations and debates, and enthused by the approach of all the voices cited above. But, for me, as an undergraduate of Sociology in the mid-1960s, the curriculum for my course was out of date and lacking in critical analysis, incapable of offering a contemporary orientation and appropriate methodologies, for example Critical Theory, to actually address these transitions, continuity and change, and the consequences for everyday life. Another Sociologist of my generation sums this up well;

'In some ways language is far too subtle a tool to be used for simply things. There at least three 'forms' of lived experience that must enter into a sociologist's work; that of those studies, the relationship between himself and those he studies as it is lived by both, and his own relationship to his ideas. The way in which he lives what he is saying, and his use of language, if sensitive and conscious, is capable of conveying something of all three. In addition, he is trying to communicate with whoever might read him...' (Craib 1998 p,125)

The staleness and conformity of conventional British Sociology (a lot of 'bean counting' went on) was thrown in to sharp relief by the work of those pioneers cited above, all of whom came from 'outside' of established, and establishment academic Sociology. One of the main concerns I had with the Sociology curriculum I encountered was the lack of any broader historical dimension to understanding the political and cultural struggles associated with everyday life and social change.

The upheavals in higher education in 1968 in particular, in the UK and beyond, emphasised the inadequacy of our academic lives compared to the radical and revolutionary spirit of the times. The challenge to the status quo in general did of course manifest itself on the campus. I recall the enthusiasm of Perry Anderson, the editor of New Left Review, the leading radical/ Marxist intellectual journal, in devoting a complete issue of the Review to the campus upheaval. Of course the radical reappraisals in the Humanities starting with F.R.Leavis, and developed by Hoggart and Williams et al, did make a significant contribution towards the questioning. Neither should we forget the creation and publication of the May Day Manifesto in 1968, edited by Raymond Williams, Stuart Hall and E.P. Thompson, a collaborative statement on the inadequacies of the Labour government led by Harold Wilson.

For many of us, especially so those engaged in radical politics and 'the arts', this was a lifeline;

'Cultural sociology…is concerned with the social processes of all cultural production, including those forms of production which can be designated as ideologies' (Williams 1981 p.30)

There is no doubt in my mind that the relative failure of the 1968 events did result in a much greater focus on formulating questions and answers on the role of culture in everyday life, and as suggested elsewhere in this essay, including the realisation of the conservative nature of much of this. This in turn emphasised the need to explore and focus upon much more the role of ideology and hegemony. This change of direction from the barricades to scholarship, educational work and curriculum development could be seen as a diversion. I have already discussed Williams argument about the semi-autonomous position of 'culture' with the historic 'base (economic) and superstructure (political)' arguments. Williams and others sought to reframe arguments around the value of cultural creativity as a mediating influence. This position on the value of the cultural arts does chime with Herbert Marcuse in the 'the truth of art lies in its power to break the monopoly of established reality to define what is real. I would also quote here Milan Kundera, from his 1986 book 'The Art of the Novel;

WRITING AND TALKING
ABOUT CULTURE

'A novel examines not reality but existence, and existence is not what has occurred, existence is the realm of human possibilities, everything that man can become, everything he's capable of. Novelists draw up the map of existence by discovering this or that human possibility. But again, to exist means: "being in the world". Thus both the character and his world must be understood as possibilities.'

For more on 1968 and the development of a cultural studies, see Tony Dunn in David Punter.

I moved from studying in Bristol to Oxford in 1969 to widen my sociological and philosophical horizons, not through the particular study of sociology or philosophy, but through researching and writing a thesis on 'The Secularist Movement in London in the 1860s'. The creation of The National Secularist Society in 1866 amounted to the highpoint of the Freethought Movement which had its origins in the Seventeenth Century English Civil War. Radical and democratic groups within the Parliamentary cause developed their ideas and aims through The Levellers, The Ranters, and the Diggers. The Protestant, and secular impetus for 'Freethinking' was carried through to the Chartist Movement of the 1830/40s and beyond in to Secularism, Socialism and Republicanism in the later Nineteenth Century.

I have fond memories of spending my first term in Oxford reading many Nineteenth Century novels, and radical journals 'heavy' with cultural inferences, references, and cultural nuances. So, although I was not 100% sure then that what I was doing was creating a cultural study, in Williams' terms a 'structure of feeling', that was in fact exactly what I was doing! The myriad of cultural highways and byways that was in the collective consciousness of those advocates of freethought and secularism had a considerable influence on my thinking and writing;

'We write history not only to clarify, and codify personal assessments of past life; but eventually to pass on some comments for general dissemination and criticism' (Astley 1969)

So, in my mind, there is no doubt that the work of Williams et al did create a 'cultural turn' within Sociology, including an approach to what is called 'close reading' of texts, fiction and non-fiction, in order to gain a greater understanding of the motives of the author in drawing our attention key issues. This 'reading' can also give us an understanding of the day to day conditions of practice for that writer, which can give us, the reader a greater insight in to their creativity.

Amongst others fields of interest Williams is talking about the Media in all its forms, forms of cultural production very deliberately focused on 'cultural thought-washing'.

Williams adds;

'A sociology of culture must concern itself with the institutions and formations of cultural production...' (Williams 1981 p.30)

This approach led to the concept of 'cultural materialism', real social things including human labour. This argument then leads us in to a long running debate about the relationship between 'social being', us as material beings, and 'social consciousness', what we think. However, we must keep reminding ourselves that theory, any theory about anything let alone culture, does not exist in a vacuum. All theories and the creative processes of theorising, by real flesh and blood human beings, has a context, has motives, for good and for ill.

Another key issue here, to which I will return later, emphasises the argument about the creative 'making' of a culture argued by Edward Thompson, mentioned above. He argued that the creative process of this 'making' was a self- conscious recognition by the emergent industrial working class culturally, and was a recognition of themselves as a class in themselves, leading to them understanding and fashioning themselves as a class for themselves, a political entity.

Following Williams' lead on coming to understand the cultural dimension of material objects when linked to people, can take us to some interesting places and discussions. For example, here is Hanna Laikola, a leading Finnish designer;

'Empathy in design describes the ability to have a deeper understanding and to put yourself in another person's shoes to truly see the world through their eyes. As a designer, it goes beyond the superficial, aesthetic or what something looks like. We have to change our mind set to build empathy at every opportunity – so. Getting to know your user's feelings as if they were your own. However, I also think the user should understand why an object or space was designed the way it was. When both sides have a better understanding, we can apply and use empathy to make smart design decisions in the future.' (Laikola 2022)

The real 'cultural turn' here, connecting the aesthetic with the utilitarian, with human sensibilities added in.

It was around this time of 'the cultural turn' that my own ideas on the scope, reach and powerful influence of the Media were taking shape, and my development of the concept, 'Ideological Cultural Apparatuses'(ICAs). Let me quote myself from 2008 on ICAs;

'...the everyday mechanisms by which our commonplace and regularly used ideas, images and values are recycled for our endless "entertainment", or titillation. Here we are flattered, have our strings pulled, and generally praise ourselves for being so clever; hedonism and solipsism combined in self actualisation! We are, of course, constantly on the cusp of consuming some new, and essential, thing; another example in this age of information of more knowledge without wisdom' (Astley 2008 p.13)

I will say more about this later, for example when discussing nationalism and myth making, but for now would add that a good deal of critical and Marxist theory had continued to emphasise how State apparatuses, like schooling and education more broadly, had set out to control and limit the creative and alternative thinking of people, young and older. Available and disseminated Knowledge was what the Establishment, the ruling classes, had decided was appropriate, regardless of the everyday life experience of the majority of people. My argument was then, and still being so, that the power of the tightly controlled, and mainly commercial Media had in fact become the greatest threat to truth.

Ideology

To clarify, this is what I mean by ideology, the ability of certain small groups of powerful owners and managers of the media, education and so on to impose their vested interests, their view of the world, through the control of ideas, information and images. They want to dictate what is our culture, and feel entitled to do so.

Williams, like many others who will be cited, also wrote about that 'everyday life experience' and coined the concept 'structure of feeling' already mentioned, to sum up his thoughts on the messiness, complexity, and often unselfconsciousness, of such lived experience;

'The term I would suggest to describe it is structure of feeling: it is as firm as 'structure' suggests, yet it operates in the most delicate and least tangible parts of our activity. In one sense, this structure of feeling is the culture of a period: is the particular living result of all the elements in the general organization. And it is in this respect that the arts of a period, taking these to include characteristic approaches and tones in argument, are of major importance' (Williams 1965 p.64/65)

One aspect of discussing 'everyday life', is coming to terms with both the ubiquity of our lives, shared as they are with so many others; but also the biographical particularity of our own life, one not exactly lived by anyone else. To cite Lefebvre citing Hegel, 'the familiar is not necessarily the known'! Williams also emphasises the research, and research methods issues here when he talks about 'knowable communities'.

Sociologists do have the concept of 'social capital' which emphasises the connections between people in a locality, and/or a culture group, usually based on the shared needs of those people, and the historical responses to need and problem solving. Social Capital emphasises that there exists within culture groups a reservoir of knowhow to be drawn on as required. Reciprocity and trust is central to this concept, highlighting the idea that cooperation has many practical and emotional benefits. The creation of The Cooperative and Trade Union Movements in the mid nineteenth century an obvious example. These social bonds are cultural, and act as a bulwark against the tendency in an individualist and wage based economy, and addresses the isolation that comes from the alienating effects of a money driven, and a here today and gone tomorrow society. A snakes and ladders existence of precariousness.

As I discuss throughout this essay community is a mental construct, symbolising the past and the invention of tradition. This is often a necessary precaution for an often inward looking culture group meeting needs in line with what I have argued above. This symbolic world is powerful and emphasises how we use symbols in everyday life to stand for, or suggests something else by reason of association or convention, a visible, or spoken sign of something invisible, or so taken for granted, that it is rendered invisible. Of course, these symbols are known to some, the insiders, but not by others, this is largely their purpose. But at all times interpretation is evident, and incursions in to the relatively secure world on the culture group can be disrupted by 'cultural invaders'. Are those social bonds strong enough to resist emergent assaults on the homogeneity of the 'structure of feeling'? An issue that Richard Hoggart emphasised in 'Uses of Literacy'.

Many social and cultural critics have argued that the myth of the individual as the only viable successful human condition has been pervasive. We can all make our own way in life, the pioneer spirit and so on. There is no such thing as 'society' as Margaret Thatcher infamously claimed, we should all pursue our own interests, constantly in competition with others for scarce resources of all kinds. When in doubt the 'market' solve our personal problems on the road to embracing possessive individualism. In fact, we know that this isolationist way of life tends to create loneliness and vulnerability. Social Capital argues the value, to one and all, of inter-connectivity as a way of life.

David Vincent in his book 'Literacy and Popular Culture' (1989) quotes the anthropologist Geertz that culture is the 'informal logic of actual life'; give our situation, it makes sense. This may be particularly important if we are trying to understand the lives of people in the past whose world view, their sense and sensibilities were often very different from ours. For example, up to two hundred years or so ago, most people grew up with and lived their lives within powerful religious cultures. That was the daily context to their lives, to the framework of their thinking, and also to what, if they were literate, their reading.

I grew up in a different, but in many ways similar context, increasingly turning to the burgeoning popular cultures of my teens in the late 1950s/1960s to think and act differently, contrarily. Once the post 1945 liberal values oriented social democratic welfare state-ism opened the Pandora's box of primarily commercially driven, style creating alternative narratives of everyday life, there was no going back despite all the harrumphing!

The so-called 'generation gap' of the 1960s simply represented the gulf between us; with a narrative of 'our own', and them, the other. Everything from being 'Free', to music, to hair, to clothes, to lifestyle, sexual mores, to who controls the curriculum of higher education, was up for debate. And we did debate; that was a radical shift in the nature of a 'structure of feeling', a way of seeing and doing. These all became both the sight of struggle and sites of struggle. Revolt in to Style! Through inhabiting that culture we became newly aware of ourselves, making sense of ourselves.

Not cohesive, or comprehensive, or, in many ways, lasting, but it did shape a lot of us, by for example taking many 60s graduates in to the public sector to work, in order to help build that better, fairer, more socially just society. This was for us at least a key element in 'the long revolution'. We became a thinking and active part of that whole, that 'structure of feeling'. That has lasted in my generation despite all the desires and temptations to reject it

Having raised the nature and role of 'popular culture' I will add a few more

50

comments here, and return later.

'Popular culture…is that culture which expresses the aesthetic, ideological, hedonistic, spiritual, and symbolic values of a particular group of people; we can read those values in popular practices, texts and objects…say a TV as "popular television" not because of its viewing figures, nor because of its producers' marketing tactics, but because of its formal qualities, its aesthetic strategies, its organisation of pleasure.' (Frith 1997 p.416)

Simon Frith is a Sociologist who has specialised in the study of popular music, and emphasises here the idea that tastes vary for access to information, education and entertainment. Those tastes, individually and collectively, are largely the consequence of our being the member of a culture group for whom those choices are related to identity. We know what we like, and selections are made from the ever growing range of cultural products and experiences. Seeking pleasure is certainly a major factor in those choices. There are 'high' and 'low' culture issues here in who says what is popular or minority tastes. In the 'Uses of Literacy', Richard Hoggart emphasised that even in the 1950s, that market place of choices was already considerable, especially for cultural entertainment products from the USA and made mainly negative comparisons with the indigenous 'folk' culture of the time, place and class etcetera. As already mentioned I was exposed to that growing new world of life style choices. Of course the extent to which any one of us decides to draw on the outpourings of this popular culture; therefore, making it even more popular; reflects the strength or weakness of the dominant value system and social controls associated with our everyday life culture. We were not 'sponges' simply soaking up the latest fashion in the market place, we did place our own interpretations on what we heard and saw; did this meet our needs and aspirations? Was it about us, the key cultural interests of our peer group? I grew up in a liberal, and open minded family, and my parents did not object to my enthusiasm for, and engagement with 'new' music, clothes, and entertainment choices that I made. Perhaps I also knew the limits of their forbearance? They bequeathed to me my cultural 'inheritance'. My cultural capital.

It was in the 1960s that Sociologists were focusing much more on the concept of cultural capital, which briefly suggests that the educational benefits, and much else besides, bestowed upon us by the culture that we as an individual grew up in. Our socialisation with attendant social controls, is like money in the bank. Schools in the UK have been dominated by middle class values and language, and therefore if a child lives that life at home, is what is replicated at school. This bodes well for academic achievement and finding a place in the privileged sections of later life. This is usually linked with a family status network which shares this know-how of the 'system' and can exploit those familiarities. This in turn leads to an increasing emphasis on the accumulation of human capital, our personal CV offering, that enables up to more successful in entering the labour market and maintain the status from which we have come. Our acquisition of possessive individualism is complete.

Another important dimension of cultural capital is in the endless arguments about knowledge and historical truth. What constitutes historical truth, and how we know that it is so at any time is affected by, and in turn effects, contemporary fashions. Take for example the common place enthusiasm for all things 'artisan', 'shabby-chic' and 'retro-chic' in general. Can you discern the fine line between authenticity and marketing bullshit? Nostalgia reigns supreme; the last refuge of those who have a sense of hope for the good society lost, and an apathy, a laziness to actually do anything political about it. Raphael Samuel raised this historical conundrum when discussing 'unofficial knowledge', and for example oral history;

'Popular memory is on the face of it the very antithesis of written history. It eschews notions of determination and seizes instead on omens, portents and signs. It measures change genealogically, in terms of generations rather than centuries, epochs or decades. It has no developmental sense of time, but assigns events to the mythicized 'good old days (or bad old days) of workplace lore, or the 'once upon a time' of the storyteller,' (Samuel 1994 p.6)

IDEOLOGY

I discuss elsewhere the importance of nostalgia in the public consciousness, an individual and collective driver of a longing for a more secure and recognisable past. Something that advertisers for example have exploited. But, as I have argued memories are part of that residual culture, an important aspect of cultures that act as a glue, conservative though they might often be. Walter Benjamin (1892- 1940) a significant cultural critic, and member of the Frankfurt School of Critical Theorists, emphasised the importance of memory for the psychology of those living in the Modern world. As with Freud, Benjamin argued that memory was potentially an emancipating force because those looking to the future most use the past as a benchmark, to understand and learn from the nature and motive forces of social change. In the nineteenth century and since, William Morris is often accused of 'living in the past', but this is not true as his concern was to understand the fact and fiction, myths, of the past in order to deal with the present and the future. Morris' understanding of society and arts and crafts of 'the past' directed his own work in design, arts practice and the role of human labour in an industrial capitalist world.

I must add here to what I have said already about the importance of community and indigenous cultures. There has been a hundred year plus debate about the impact of industrial capitalism and urbanisation. In the nineteenth century Tonnies, the German Sociologist argued that social relations changed dramatically away from organic community to self-centred individualism, the age of the wage labourer, 'association'. 'All that is solid melts into air', which is notoriously difficult to grasp, over whelming and chaotic. In the 1930s Leavis the literally critic argued that what mattered from a humanistic perspective was the promotion of the organic, a morally and culturally conservative outlook. So, for all the talk of the 'everlasting' value of the indigenous, the known, culture, is this essentially a negative, backward looking answer to the demands of living in a carnivorous industrial capitalism?

Morris like Benjamin and others have questioned the inaccuracy of

53

assuming that the characteristics of industrial capitalism ensures progress or civilisation.

'Resistance' via nostalgia makes for a good story, and clearly there is no shortage of ideas and practice that value just this. And, in the grand all things to all people media world, we are not short of stories, and the fact that we all have a narrative to deliver.

On the role of the media in our lives

It is quite clear that all media actively in use in our everyday lives has changed in the last thirty years because the technology available at any one time has been transformed by both newer technology and increasing access to a vast range of programming. The digitalisation of TV in particular has been considerable along with the diversity of ways in which people obtain a signal to then actually access and consume content. The considerable growth in streaming services is an example. So, the form of all media has changed, but the relationship between owners, producers and consumers has remained much the same. Certainly access choices have changed, but whether that has had much impact on content is doubtful. Enjoyment without power other than the income and taste related choice of consuming.

Essentially TV has been a domestic medium, consumed within the family domain in one configuration or another. 'Families' did of course sit together to listen to radio (or the 'wireless' as it was usually known). It is clear that the appearance and growth of TV from the commercialisation in the mid-1950s, entered in to family life at a time when social and cultural life was already in transition; changes in locality, family life, work, education and so on. The impact of TV on everyday life is a key issue discussed below.

In their book 'Culture First!: promoting standards in the new media age' (2020) Kenneth Dyson and Walter Homolka discuss the implications of both technological changes and concentrations of ownership on a global scale;

'Culture First! Argues that the proper study of culture is normative (the normal way); and that the proper, and neglected, purpose of cultural studies should be the nurturing of …argument and judgement. The purpose can be better pursued if we return to the distinction between our "best self" and our "ordinary self" when thinking about cultural questions; if we seek to articulate and think rigorously about aesthetic and ethical standards; and if we recognize the specific cultural values of the printed word and reading as an activity and that the printed word is more than a medium, provided by a publisher.'

These authors are very clear about declining standards, and that those who know that should be in the vanguard of challenging this situation now. I have already said a good deal about why and how writers like Hoggart and his contemporaries embarked on their own challenges in the 1950s and 1960s, and in everyday life and culture circumstances many individuals and groups embarked on their own 'counter-culture' opposition to the status quo, within this rapidly changing symbolic world.

Before developing the arguments above I feel it would be valuable for the reader to have a brief consideration of cultural policy making and makers in recent years. The following passage is drawn from my 2020 monograph 'Tragedy in our everyday lives: the role of popular culture'. One of the main reasons for including this material is to consider the recent writing of Robert Hewison, his 2014 book 'Cultural Capital: the rise and fall of creative Britain'. Hewison has been a prolific contributor to the ongoing debates about the role of the arts and cultural policy in the UK. Apologies in advance for any necessary overlaps with other sections of my essay.

Cultural policy; practice and power

By the mid-1960s increasing numbers of working families buoyed by higher incomes, often as a consequence of more wives/mothers working, looked to their aspirational values being providing by the market place, and less so by the local and national State apparatus. Of course there were still many working families for whom the 'social wage'; the term conventionally given to the monetary value of care, benefits and services; was still essential for an improved quality of life. But, personal consumption in the growing marketplace did expand rapidly resulting in a set of values linked to possessive individualism rather than traditional cultural supports. (Hall 1988)

New forms of popular culture, including advertising, increasingly carried by TV, expanded alongside growth in the marketplace. One of the bitter ironies of this rush to the market, the exponential growth in the demand for goods, was the calculated choice by corporations to move the manufacture of many goods to the 'Third World', where labour costs were much lower. The 'popular culture' of strong trade unions, this collective control mechanism, pushed up wages; eventually jobs would be lost, while profits were maintained. This is an issue that keeps being addressed in this essay.

When the Labour government, led by Tony Blair, came to office in 1997, they set about tidying up State policy on the relationship between the Arts, Heritage, the Media and economic development, whether through the market place for the Arts, or tourism and the hospitality industry.

The Government Department of Culture, Media and Sport was created with Chris Smith as the first Secretary of State. In 1998 a creative industries taskforce produced the Creative Industries Mapping Document in 1998, which set done the State's definition; 'those industries which have their origin in individual creativity, skill and talent which have a potential for job and wealth creation through the generation and exploitation of intellectual property.' DCMS 1998.

Keep the 'exploitation' in mind here, another version of the mantra that there is no human activity that cannot be turned in to money making opportunity.

DCMS identified thirteen industry sectors, ranging from advertising to broadcasting, with all the 'creative' arts along the way. The very definition cited above merely reinforces the existence of the age old tension between aesthetics, purpose, utility, and the market place. Every artist has their price!

The DCMS represented an updating of State Cultural Policy. The post 1945 years in the UK had seen an expansion of the desire by successive governments do democratise access to what was considered to be 'high value' art/cultural artefacts. The Arts Council had been created in 1946 to both

57

show that the State understood that 'the arts' were a social good, and that more/most people should be given the opportunity to see, understand and engage. This ethos was much in line with the contemporaneous creation of the 'Welfare State' which also sought to administer in to existence a range of care, benefits and services that improved the standard and living and quality of life of most people. Access to 'the arts' was a social good like having health, free at the point of delivery and so on. As always these policies were very much about compensating most people in the UK, who could not otherwise enter in to the market place to buy to meet their needs.

There would of course be limits on how much the State would wish to spend, and there would be regulation to ensure that standards were met, and that the ordinary folk should not be exposed to anything that their betters considered would not be a 'social or private good'.

As the influence of market forces has increased since the 1940s; for example, the State allowing commercial broadcasting to 'compete' with the BBC; has caused many problems for government of the day to control and regulate exactly what people are exposed to. Once the Pandora's Box was opened the ability of the State to regulate has been become tested creating a situation where the State appears to be constantly catching up with new developments, including new technologies and globalisation of trade and cultural artefacts. Controlling people's behaviour continues to be problematic. Whose agency are we talking about, when for example, a re-orientated cultural focus has been transformed by a less gender specific multi-culturalism?

Hoggart's book was in fact one of many contributions to the on-going, but suddenly very urgent, discussion about the nature and effects of Popular Culture, i.e. all the new-ish, and rapidly expanding 'mass media of communications'. Liberal minded members of the Educational establishment were very anxious about the way in which the values that they held true were being undermined, seen as irrelevant, and replaced in the common consciousness by the widespread consumption of this new ephemera. As I say later, the politicians of the 1950s and early 1960s felt impelled to find out what on earth was going on, and respond accordingly through regulation and social controls. Popular Culture was a problem! An expanding, more socially and politically aware TV began to incorporate the radical trends happening in the theatre. And, while much small scale, and niche theatre could be ignored, what appeared on TV screens could not. Ironically, the lack of choice for TV watchers in the 50s and 60s meant their increasing exposure to 'new' drama.

As TV consumers, we all take actions, but not necessarily in conditions of our own choosing. And while many people did sign up for the bright new consumer culture, and saw this as a positive move towards a less class bound society, a 're-making' of social status and opportunity, not everyone did, or could, share this new freedom. Some of the best examples of popular culture in the late 1950s and 1960s brought this paradox to our attention.

But, the rise in so called identity politics is evident here, what Raymond Williams referred to as a militant particularism, allied to the growth of possessive individualism I discuss in this essay. This has certainly had an impact on the appeal, or lack of, a socialist politics that foregrounds the collective over the individual. The Labour Party has consistently struggled with this phenomenon!

Arthur Miller discussed this line of argument in his 1949 article for The New York Times in 1949;

'Tragedy enlightens – and it must, in that it points the heroic finger at the enemy of man's freedom. The thrust for freedom is the quality in tragedy which exalts. The revolutionary questioning of the stable environment is what terrifies. In no way is the common man debarred from such thoughts or such actions.' (Quoted in Dukore 1974)

Miller went on to emphasise the crucial role of the 'writer' in that the creative impulse must understand and assert the consequences of cause and effect. The character of the hero, woman or man, drives them forward to seek their goal, their humanity regardless of the apparently impossible odds. The death of the king, or the death of a salesman?

The importance of a dialectical approach is also essential here because the conflicting arguments confronting the heroic person must be changed by historical events in to a synthesis, an outcome, for good or for ill. Tensions must be resolved, the story line completed, within the timeframe of the production and the scheduling. This destiny is essential to the action in whatever form that is creatively portrayed.

The combination of having something serious to say, and the articulation to say it, reminds me of C.Wright Mills, and contemporary of Miller, emphasising the writer's 'vocabulary of motives'.

In his book 'Modern Tragedy' Raymond Williams emphasised the importance of this historical dimension;

'My central argument...was on the deep relations between the actual forms of our history and the tragic forms within which these are perceived, articulated and reshaped.What I ...note is a strengthening of one of these forms, which in cultures like my own has become temporarily dominant and indeed, at times, overwhelming.

In its most general sense this can be expressed, simply, as a widespread loss of the future.' (Williams 1979 p.207/8)

Williams sought to emphasise the connected meanings in our lives, which can be revealed through dramatic representation. Tragedy can be seen to expose for our examination the continuous sense of life, but by no means taking place in a neat straight line.

Williams is here discussing what I have mentioned above, that the reliance by people on the continuance of a liberal democratic society fuelled by the post 1945 social democratic ideology, the 'post-war' settlement of a state led collective context to everyday life. This orthodox world view of thirty years standing, was however, too shallowly planted in to the political soil of social and economic life, and by the late 1970s all too easily swept away by the rise of a hard-nosed money led neo-liberalism. The State had shaped and managed this progressive infrastructure, assuring 'the people' that they would continue to be looked after, but, the people were not sufficiently in control of this destiny.

Writing in 1961, Raymond Williams acknowledged the complexity of any analysis of our diverse everyday cultural life;

'We need to distinguish three levels of culture, even in its most general definition. There is the lived culture of a particular time and place, only fully accessible to those living in that time and place. There is the recorded culture, of every kind, from art to the most everyday facts: the culture of a period. There is also, as the factor connecting lived culture and period cultures, the culture of the selective tradition.' (Williams 1961 in Bennett p.49)

But whose culture we are discussing, even celebrating, remains a key issue. And reinforced by Paul Willis in his 1970 book 'Common Culture'. As Williams argued TV watching has a 'flow', one programme after another, with usually no logical reason for this, but all watched! I recall watching the surreal final episode of Alan Bleasdale's 'Boys from the Blackstuff', which was immediately followed by live football from Liverpool.

In many ways the generation of dramatists that sought to transform the genre in the 1950s/60s were part of a structure of feeling, a commitment to a new medium, a politically unstable period, and a commitment to a radical intervention. I will say more about this later.

The third of Williams' levels above is what I am emphasising as the way in which 'artists' tell us stories about our pasts, present, and possible futures, even utopian ones. And, of course, as Williams argues, this is selective, the cultural canon, the conventional. The point is who makes this selection, and for what purpose?

But before we get to a discussion of what cultural practice can do, might do, we need to reinforce the point that most 'art' is still elitist in both the ideas that exist conventionally about what it is, and also who it is for. Paul Willis cited above says;

'The institutions and practices, genres and terms of high art are currently categories of exclusion more than inclusion. They have no real connection with most young people or their lives. They may encourage some artistic specializations but they certainly discourage much wider and more general symbolic creativity... If some things count as "art", the rest must be non-art'. Because "art" is in the "art gallery", it can't therefore be anywhere else. It is that which is special and heightened, and not ordinary and everyday.' (Willis 1990 in Gray p.206)

Also in Gray's book (1993), Nicholas Garnham reinforces what I argue about the nature and role of the culture industries. My discussion below, of Ideological Cultural Apparatuses (ICAs) shares with Garnham the insistence that these 'arts industries' are essentially the same as any other industrial entity in contemporary society. And as already mentioned one major difference is of course the economics of the everyday existence for arts organisations; galleries, theatres, performing companies, the BBC and so on. The role of subsidy has conventionally and contemporaneously relied on State subsidy in addition to other forms of income like Lottery money and sponsorship. And, the influence of the commercial sector in the everyday lives of people in 'the arts', individuals and organisations, was ever present. By the 1980s a whole generation of creative people had accustomed themselves to this reality.

The significance of the National Lottery for culture and cultural change cannot be ignored. John Major created this institution in 1993, which fed in to the 'get rich quick' fantasies of ordinary working people while funding the arts, a wonderful swindle dressed up as a way of subsidy. After 1979 Thatcher, and her associates, set about changing both the economic base of the UK, and the prevailing culture. The Labour government under Callaghan had emptied out the last remnants of the post 1945 prevalence of the social democratic ideology of collectivism. Thatcher & co. set about the task of changing the political narrative to one of individualism and free choice in the market place. The playwright, David Edgar said;

'...this deft sleight of hand is reflected in the actual processes of change: the brilliance of Thatcher is not...in its economics but rather in its politics, or, even ratherer, in its capacity to pursue political ends by fiscal means, to express essentially social objectives in political language, to achieve economic goals by way of a transformation of culture.' (Edgar 1988 p.13)

Edgar is discussing political dominance through a changed culture. The so-called neo-liberals, Thatcher, and up to and including Blair and Brown after 1997, had to find a way to steer the national conversation away from the dominance of the State in matters of funding, to one where these matters of subsidy would be left to the Market. Even when the Blair/Brown government did insist on the need for increased funding of the arts, the actual money was subjected to a cost/benefit set of rules.

Edgar's 1988 argument was shared by Robert Hewison in 2014;

'There is a popular prejudice that politics and the arts should not have too much to do with each other; yet they have important things in common. They are both ways of making meaning. They are concerned with values, engage the emotions, and try to change minds.' (Hewison 2014 p.3)

Blair put the arts, the 'creative industries', at the centre of his extension of the Thatcherite pre-eminence of the Market to provide all;

'Creative Britain needed a creative economy in order to ensure the continuous innovation on which growth depended. This would be served by a "creative class" whose occupation was the production of signs and symbols that could be consumed in commodified form.' (Hewison 2014 p.5)

Cultural policy became an essential part of economic policy for regeneration. I take up this local context to arts policy later in the essay when discussing my involvement in Arts And Culture East Devon (ACED).

The message to the creative arts was clear, we can arrange for you to have the money you need, but, only by our rules! No surprises then that the title of Hewison's book is 'Cultural Capital'.

Indeed, the issues about 'culture' and money that Hewison raises, emphasises the importance of the 'creative industries' to successive governments. As I discuss elsewhere in this essay, the whole idea of seeing the work and output of 'creatives' in society as the best big economic opportunity, and money making scheme, hopefully filling the gap left from the decline of manufacturing, has many critics. The degradation of 'the arts' as a consequence of being shackled to a commercial sector take-over has never worn well with a significant section of the liberal-artistically inclined population.

Blair and Brown most certainly embraced the advent of 'Cool Britannia' from the Thatcher years, and 'talked-up' a new creative Britain under the auspices of New Labour after 1997. However, the 'culture vultures' as described by Elliott and Atkinson in their 2007 book 'Fantasy Island', were prone to exaggerate the size and economic significance of the 'creative industries';

'A large number of people work in the creative industries, broadly defined, although not nearly as many as the hype would suggest. There are three times as many people working in domestic service as there are in advertising, television, video games, film, the music business and design combined; the creative industries represent around one in 20 of the people working in

Britain today. Between them they account for around 4 per cent of all UK exports of goods and services...it is hard to make serious money.' (Elliott and Atkinson 2007 p.88)

On the arts funding issue since the much enthused about extra money for the arts by Blair and Brown, it is true that in recent years there has been an attempt to spread funding more generally across community based arts activity, and the various forms of the Arts Council are making limited inroads in to the considerable imbalance between the 'big-hitters' of the arts world, and everyone else seeking subsidy. Garnham also reminds us that all of this money finding its way to worthy recipients seeks to embrace the unique importantance of 'the artist' as distinct from the grass-roots practitioner or audience.

It is also true that organisations like the Gulbenkian Foundation have encouraged liberal minded managers of arts institutions, like galleries for example, to find more innovative ways for members of the public; arty or otherwise; to gain access to the substantial resources held in trust by these institutions. Because most people, even those who do occasionally enter an art gallery, or attend the subsidised theatre, those special kinds of people who should have an entitlement to this often public money being used for private purposes, do not see themselves as 'artists'. Identity is most certainly an issue here, whether top-down or bottom-up.

So, having considered many key issues around Cultural Policy, I must now return to the role of 'cultural studies', in studying more specific areas of culture developed by sociologists of the 'working class community' like Phil Cohen (1972/1990/1997). He explored the vitality of the symbolic world of young people who emphasised the way different youth cultures groups, like Teddy Boys, The Mods, and then Skinheads, responded to their lack of economic and political power by 'dressing up', by being oppositional and deviant in the face of being discounted and demonised with those in power, aided and abetted of course by the moralising media; As Stan Cohen said, 'folk devils and moral panics'. (Cohen 1973) Agency is a key issue here where people of all ages, but often, and especially, young people, will not only understand their low status and alienation, but will act creatively in these 'sites of struggle'; sites and sights of creativity and resistance, both individually and collectively via peer groups and social media. Often with a willing suspension of the commitment to conformity. Something of those 'signifying practices' I mentioned earlier. A further example of the 'rituals of mutuality'. These symbol laden responses acknowledge that while choices may be limited, opportunities will be fashioned (quite literally) to demonstrate an alternative narrative. There is a tension here between the necessities of everyday life, a utility, and an imaginative adapting, an argot like style. Style as in the 'space' rescued, recovered from the routine, and refashioned in to something material of the self and culture group. In that style space creativity and iconoclastic transformation happens. The free development of each is the free development of all!

There is also an element here of a response by (young) people to the unfairness of their condition. The term 'moral economy' has been used by social historians and others, to argue that people do respond to the immorality of power being used to deprive them of a decent livelihood. And, as emphasised by Paul Willis, discussed in this essay, have a 'grounded' aesthetics.

In the Preface to my book on The Beatles, mentioned elsewhere in this essay, I emphasised that enduring inter-relation between the everyday experience of social institutions, our own culture group, and biography. It is real persons that are doing the social interacting, and not simply, or abstractly, their cultural forms of stylistic representations. There are psychological issues here. It may well be that the form the takes is shaped, influenced or determined by certain cultural factors at any time. Indeed, as I wrote in my chapter 'Youth' in the Beatles book, acknowledges these in questions of identity life 'apprenticeships', the investment of self, and social accountability high on the agenda. In the totality of all these factors, young people are social beings.

As I discuss in this essay the choices of service providers, and content, that are the contemporary norm has taken us as a media consuming society well beyond the terrestrial and analogue. But, who controls the technology, and what difference has the vast amount of programming actually add up to? After the introduction of commercial TV in the mid-1950s (The Conservative Party were determined to break the BBC's monopoly) there was a high level of anxiety about the effects on children and young people of watching TV. Studies were carried out by psychologists and Social-psychologists, and then by Sociologists over a period of twenty years, who in the main argued that watching TV rarely changed, but usually reinforced most people's beliefs and behaviour. This would suggest that what people had already 'knew' from their cultural life remained much the same. However, researchers did consistently demonstrate that those in control of programming did tend to assume a one size fits all approach, and for good or ill that tendency did, until quite recently, create a 'national' audience, a homogenising process. I do not feel that this is still the case, and in any way also the extent to which people were ever culturally passive consumers in the past is questionable.

One way in which we know about all these concerns about our contemporary situation and future prospects is via the media's everyday outpourings, so much of which is not only money-profit driven, but banal and vulgar into the bargain. The abuse of such sophisticated technologies puts our cultures into 'negative equity'.

'Never before in human history has so much cleverness been used to such stupid ends. The cleverness is in the creation and manipulation of markets, media and power; the stupid ends are in the destruction of community, responsibility, morality, art, religion, and the natural world.'

This is Ivo Mosley in Dumbing Down: culture politics and the Mass Media (2000). I am reminded that this kind of criticism is not new, recalling, for example, that Berthold Brecht once referred to (Hollywood) commercial movies as 'laxatives of the soul'.

As I have already suggested one of the issues that do inevitably arise from asking these is, who has the power to manipulate information, ideas, images, news, the everyday stuff of life? I will return to this question in more detail below when discussing ideology and hegemony, but it needs to be said here that the media have been regularly, and conveniently perhaps,'brainwashing' the consumers of 'the media'. As long ago as 1957 the American (and that is important to our understanding of the Britain) Vance Packard wrote 'The Hidden Persuaders', an account of mass-persuasion, with a focus on the unconscious. The opening up of this line of argument partly happened in a reaction to the prevailing liberal humanism in the USA and our national culture that did not seek to attribute such blame. However, Cultural Studies in all its guises, and incorporating all the critical theories emerging in the twentieth century, has purposely problematized the whole range of relationships between production and consumption. One line of argument is that those who own and control the means of communication; for example, Google or Rupert Murdoch; including what had been commonly described as 'the mass media', have for their own purposes sought to insidiously manipulate the substance and flow of ideas and images. These purposes might be that those in control of these means of communication feel that they have a duty to censor, control, guide and generally protect the common people from matters that are unsuitable or inappropriate. The engineering of consent through an appeal to possessive individualism. The reinforcement of consumer society, where increasing numbers of people were encouraged to see themselves as consumers first, and workers second; the means to an end. An example would be the renewed interest in our bodies, widespread amongst the middle classes. The now taken for granted obsessive focus on the self has driven ever more concerns about body image, and not just in women. We are now showered in a constant flow of ads for cosmetics, and all manner of other commodities to make us look, smell and feel better. Just one evening watching commercial television would lay bare obsessive focus on self-maintenance and improvement, the quest for endless youth and physical attractiveness; and apparently 'we are worth it', a self-fulfilling myth. This pushiness is what Raymond Williams referred to as 'militant particularism'.

68

A further example of the flashy superficiality that comes with much of media outpourings, especially so those linked with advertising., especially the 'lifestyle' stuff.

These are key issues in any discussion about who says what to whom and for what reasons, and raises the question of who has agency in their own, and the lives of other people. Clearly the influence of family, schooling, religion and so on, sit alongside the media as contenders for values manipulation for whatever reasons. And this is how we need to think about power; what does it mean? How is it manifested in everyday life? We have fairly recently entered into 'the culture wars' where certain sections of the political right (on both sides of the Atlantic) have coordinated a public relations campaign, an ideology, in this war of words over whose culture matters (including arguments over climate change). The aim is to belittle and discredit anyone who challenges the dominant white, male, conservative and powerful elites on the value of whose culture matters. The word Woke is in much use by those described above that do not believe that people's aspiration and hope to be 'woken' and treated as an equal regardless of their personal characteristics. This is where those of us who believe in equality of opportunity and freedom of speech need to make a stand against those people and organisations who feel challenged by this.

I have argued throughout this essay that diversity and variety in cultural lives and taste in not only inevitable, but to be welcomed. So again, this is where an understanding of culture, a grounded focus. comes in to its own, by which I mean an aesthetics (what is considered desirable and makes us feel good) that comes from the person, the subject themselves with the minimum of ideological persuasion. The consumption of tasteful commodities runs deep in the consciousness of people, especially so the middle classes, who have a lot to lose in making the wrong choices. There can appear to be autonomy in the choices people make, but the extent of this agency is in fact circumscribed and manipulated. If art is sublime, enters in to and reflects our 'soul', marks us out for who we are, can it survive the commodification and marketization

WRITING AND TALKING
ABOUT CULTURE

of 'art'? Not only is the sublime degraded, so are we. When thinking about the power of the art market on taste I always recall John Berger's idea that 'In life it would be better if paintings were for looking at.' (Berger 1960 p.217)

Does the dominance of monetary values stand in the way of the idealistic desire for art to reconcile humanity as we know it, with nature?

I do not intend to spend much time discussing the centuries old arguments about the analysis of our sensibility, our feelings, towards art. The reader can look this up in for example the source given here. (Payne 1997: and Eagleton 1990) What I would say now is that there is undoubtedly an ideology of aesthetics consistent with what I have said here, which ties in with my discussion of the creation, maintenance and destruction of cultures. As I have already argued, values around art; its purpose, role and value in our everyday lives is inextricably bound up with the reasoning; thinking, reactions, and reflection that people bring to their lives. Taste is more to do with the culture we live in, and more than mere personal whims. One of the key issues already raised in this essay is to ask who has the right to make judgements on art, and our relationship with it.

From a political theory perspective there are some basic truths here and to repeat myself There is no human activity that cannot be turned in to a money making opportunity by the people who wish to, and have the capacity (first and foremost the capital) to do so. The Bourgeoisie tend to use their money to make more money, thereby reinforcing their power and prestige. The Petit-Bourgeoisie (the middle classes) however spend their money on leisure, meeting their welfare needs including housing; a lot of conspicuous consumption on all domains, maintain status and trying to match their heroes the 'upper classes' hanging on to their 'coat tails' in their fawning and toadying ways. The lower orders fritter away what they have in the way of disposable income, often in a live now and pay later mentality, seduced by get-rich-quick fantasies and a wishful belief that the precarious day to day existence can actually be improved.

70

Here again is another reminder of the role of art, to enter in to these sets of relationships and 'explode' them. Dreamers awake!

There is also a major theoretical argument here (and for at least the last fifty years) about the extent to which people set free from the traditional and 'top-down' value laden constraints placed upon us, just decide to do their own, contemporary and cultural thing. Be a free-wheeling selfish consumer. A willing abandonment to the commitment to conformity. The arrival of a full blown consumer culture coincided with a growth in ideas about the sanctity of the self and freedom; a blank cheque to ignore the traditional set of rules to 'know your place' and engage with and celebrate a much more focused cultures of choice.

Elsewhere in this essay I have mentioned the ideas around postmodernism, the key ideas associated with a post-modern world, the reality that service industries have often replaced manufacturing ones in our kind of society. That 'modern' world has now been superseded. In their shared book 'Trash Aesthetics', Hinton and Kaye state that;

'Postmodernism, it has been said, means never having to say you're sorry. With the collapse of universally applicable standards of aesthetic judgement, postmodern audiences are supposedly free to make of texts pretty much what they like. No one in this whirl of cultural relativism need ever apologise for their pleasures (Hinton and Kaye in Cartmell ed. p.1)

I am sure that more people (including members of the capitalist class) believe that they cannot control the external and turbulent world, and so seek to focus on themselves, self -help with a difference. This constant turn-over in consumer and 'pop' culture makes money, lots of money, and does not require long-term investment in single products, this is 'fluid' capitalism. And, also celebrates the experience of identity without the necessity to address inconvenient moral issues about maintaining the 'canon' of taste, of standards. Any tricky issues, like for example educational values, can be left to the State apparatus to mop up.

But, as I have already argued earlier in this essay, this situation has developed over a long period of time, in fact over the period of my life time, and more importantly over the time covered by the pioneering analytical work of Hoggart, Thompson and Williams. I grew up in the era of the post 1948 creation of the 'welfare state', and, the 1950s era when Harold Macmillan could say 'You've never had it so good!' This is true and not true at the same time because the consumer led, market driven 'affluence' which many members of the old industrial working class experienced was a veneer that covered over the inability of capitalism to maintain those advances in living standards and a narrowing of the historical gap between classes. So called embourgeoisement; we are all middle class now; thesis soon unravelled as the expansion of the market could not be sustained beyond the collapse of the profound, bitter, costs of de-industrialisation. In the 1950s the Labour Party leadership actually believed the embourgeoisement myth, assuming their constituency of the traditional labour base were lost forever. And, many years later they assumed the same after the breaching of the 'red wall' seats in 2019. However, as I hope I have shown in this essay indigenous cultures are much less changed than successive years of Labour Party leadership have believed. They gave up in 1976 when the cost of welfare; care, benefits and provisions (the social wage) scared them into a much closer alliance with the idea that the market was the only hope. Social ownership (socialism) was abandoned in favour of privatisation and belief that possessive individualism would be the panacea. It is true that a clear shift to self-interest has occurred, but as Stuart Hall has argued (1988) a marked degree of 'cultural belongingness' continues despite all the pessimist predictions. The years of the Pandemic showed quite clearly that more people did rely on community support, locality self-help, a recognition of stresses and strains, and an independence of action in the face of State incompetence and indifference. This model of social enterprise drew heavily on social capital. This is also an important aspect of a 'survival culture' that has once again drawn deeply from the well of a legacy of cultural grit. However, it has been the case for many years that while the gap between the 'haves' and the have-nots' may increase a sense of fairness has prevailed. One of the reasons why the NHS has remained of a very high value for people is because it represents fairness, and despite all the talk of classlessness (and Thatcher's enthusiasm for selling off council houses epitomises this) people still feel that poverty may exist relatively, the continuation of inequality and unfairness is not acceptable. As I have argued throughout this essay consumer capitalism has lulled many people in to thinking that the gap in inequality and opportunity has narrowed, but as Jeremy Seabrook argued in the 1980s this was a key aspect of the 'Great Consumer Swindle'. Even though many individuals from working class homes; Hoggart and Storey say, had benefitted from the extent of social mobility that post 1944/5 as an aspect of the 'welfare state' and social democratic politics had provided, within twenty years, one generation, these opportunities had stopped. It is clear, then and now, that an indigenous sense of scepticism about changes has turned into a deep cynicism, not the least aspects being politics and politicians. Working class people in the 1950s and since realised that their work was a commodity, but their own culture was not. The rise and influential power of consumer capitalism has marketised their lives beyond recognition.

One further dimension to this discussion of people's relationship with their cultural 'home', is psychologically the issue of emotion, and how we come to understand and deal with the daily onslaught of expressions of emotion, for example in TV programmes, like 'Soaps'; a grotesque misrepresentation of everyday life. As Seabrook and others have asked, 'what kind of human beings are we, and what do we want to become?' A complete focus on self-interest heightens emotion, and the likelihood of emotional instabilities, argued by many people including Christopher Lasch in his 1984 book 'The Minimal Self; psychic survival in troubled times.' The road travelled by the narcissist, embracing the aura of the latest sensation. The society of the spectacle is never far away in 'the century of the self'. Some years ago school students were exposed to classes on emotional literacy in order that they would become aware of their own emotions, and how to deal with them. I am sure there are parents and teachers who would prefer children to put a cap on their shows of emotion, but the social world around them provides a different approach. As I have already argued people have increasingly become semi-detached from their indigenous culture, drawn away from their 'origins' to 'destinations' that seem more consistent and desirable with the sets of values that have come to be the drivers of everyday life and aspiration.

There is an important issue here for social science and the Humanities, about the plausibility of statements made in support of ideas like the role of cultural identity. I have already cited Richard Hoggart's as a theorist who moved between his own 'autobiographical' account of the indigenous culture that he experienced, and his generalisations from that. As I have said this way of looking appears in the work of David Storey (amongst many others like Melvyn Bragg), this autobiographical fiction reminds me of the comment made by Vico, the philosopher, that 'imagination is nothing but the working over of what is remembered'. It is clear that the 'cultural turn' in Sociology that I discussed earlier, does attempt a verisimilitude, the appearance of being true or real, because as I have just asserted the nature of looking is often what matters.

And, the creative arts do, and must play a key role in this. As I have already stressed the contribution of 'the arts' is undervalued in this society. What I have argued throughout this essay is that studying culture is one way of providing a space for more diverse and alternative voices to be heard, tell their story.

There are good reasons why people have come to look at aspects of their everyday life in a certain way. It is for people like me to explore and attempt to explain that.

By definition theses aspects of the social reconstruction of everyday life was not confined to the growing and better educated middle classes, but they were much more likely to be both the drivers and consumers of such change towards a more pluralist society. My discussion in this essay of Ideological

Cultural Apparatuses (ICAs) is important in this respect. I will consider the issues about these influences, and who 'controls' them in my chapter on Hegemony.

One of the key influences of the new 'Cultural Studies' was that it sought to shed light upon the ignored, and marginalised everyday cultural realities of a diverse range of people. The work of Williams, Hoggart and Thompson amongst other 'pioneers' was to explore the value of 'minority', and therefore less powerful, less understood, less seen, and less acknowledged people, their cultural lives, their identity. It is also important to remind ourselves that culture groups are just that, groupings, with many different factors in play such as locality and other demographic issues. There has often been a tendency to see social class groups, like the working class, or youth, to be culturally homogenous, but they are not. Extensive ethnographic studies have always emphasised diversity. And, just below the surface of these residual cultures are folk traditions, which are often oppositional. I say more about this in my section on Nationalism.

I have always used the shorthand; power + legitimacy = authority, because this emphasises the 'soft' power aspect of domination (no need for guns and tanks) that Packard was discussing in the 1950s. In 'our' national cultural values there is a conventional acceptance of hierarchy; privilege and entitlement are entrenched, for example the monarchy. As Orwell argued, who controls the past controls the future! In the opening of my 2008 book 'Herbivores and Carnivores: the struggle for democratic cultural values in post-war Britain' I said;

'As I write this, there is a good deal of discussion as to whether democracy is in decline in Britain, and if indeed there is a democratic deficit in our lives. Moreover, what is actually being mourned is not democracy, because we have never had it, but the loss of that hope we had in achieving a democratic life.'

A good deal of what I have already said emphasises the best, but perhaps,

75

second best values of indigenous cultures. People in subordinate 'classes' given their experience of life do not believe there is any likelihood of change, and therefore within reason settle for an 'ignore, adopt and adapt' approach to life, drawing on their 'own' culture for some resolution to living with identity and dignity intact? John Burnheim offers a starting point in this discussion;

'Democracy does not exist in practice. At best we have what the ancients would have called elective oligarchies with strong monarchical elements...' and as for people's reaction and response to this situation; 'And what they can do is a matter of what they have ways of doing, individually and collectively.' (my emphasis) (Burnheim 1985 p.1/2)

What appears to be the situation, and what is actually the reality as lived? As I often said to my Sociology students that the 'swinging 60s' was not swinging for everyone! The Nottingham based research 'The Forgotten Englishmen' (1970) by Coates and Silburn, and the BBC1 Play for Today 'Cathy come Home' just two examples of note.

Between Brecht and Mosley, Neil Postman had spelt out some key issues in the title of his 1985 book, 'Amusing Ourselves to Death: Public discourses in the age of Show Business.' Postman always placed considerable emphasis on the 'business' end of creativity, which links directly with what I discuss in this essay about the 'Creative Industries'. And, all of what I argue here is a constant reminder for us of the tension between an aesthetic approach to the arts compared with a variety of utilitarian ones.

So, now, taking up Mosley's argument, we need to ask ourselves some searching questions about how, and why, the media has got into the all-powerful position it has in contemporary life. Is one of the real reasons why it matters because so many otherwise apparently sensible people believe so much of what they see and hear?

In 'The Country and the City' mentioned earlier, Raymond Williams discusses the way engagement with the past is 'set up', our perceptions are managed, with historical cultural artefacts like stately homes owned by the National Trust a good example. Writers like Williams, Edward Thompson, and later in the early 1970s John Berger with 'Ways of Seeing' (TV series and book), argued that there was a political dimension to our perception of the cultural. The very title of Berger's intervention sums this up, with his deliberate ideological aim to upset the status quo of our looking. Berger showed us Gainsborough's picture 'Mr. and Mrs. Andrews', sat in their (or more likely his) grounds, their estate, grand house in the background. Mr. A with his gun and adoring gun-dog, all equipoise. However, a more historically informed observer would note that this landowner was almost certainly favoured by all the money emanating from shrewd investments in the financial markets of the City of London, even possibly the proceeds of the slave trade.

For people of all ages Berger says 'seeing comes before words'and have been taught to perceive aspects of our cultures in ways that usually promote the high value of privilege, entitlement and celebrity, while ignoring the mechanisms that allow such inequalities to exist.

Back in June 2003 Richard Hoggart wrote a piece for the Guardian, 'This is as dumb as it gets', primarily about falling standards in British TV, which could get a lot worse if large parts of production infrastructure were to be sold off to (mainly USA) companies. Channel 4's 'independence' as a State owned but advertising funded commissioner of programmes was under threat of privatisation. Sound familiar, twenty years later? Hoggart says;

'Channel 4's recent 100 Worst Britons programme was widely damned as probably the tackiest of today's huge range of trashy programmes. I remember Jeremy Isaacs, as he handed over C4, threatening severe punishment on his successors if they wrecked the channel he created. He had better get over there soon…Vapid programmes are like mild drugs; they feed on themselves. They are not part of an inert process. The appetite grows by what it feeds on.

They have increasingly to spice themselves up (so as to beat the competition, not so as to make better programmes) A further inescapable rule is that if you don't aim to do better, in any and everything, you will inevitably do worse.' (Hoggart 2003)

Part of the problem here is the sheer ubiquity of 'cultural' artefacts, consumable goods. For example, the range and fashion conscious aspect of interior design, both domestic and commercial. As Terry Eagleton says;

'The bogus populism of the commodity, its warm-hearted refusal to rank, exclude and discriminate, is based on a blank indifference to absolutely everyone'. (Eagleton 2016 p.157)

This is also true regardless of whether the commodity is a 'high' or a 'low' culture one; they all have objective as well as subjective social tendencies, they matter to the people who consume them. And if we ask Anthropologists they usually tell us that conspicuous consumption is familiar across cultures. Something will count as high or low status, and the devotees of High Culture invariably argue that their culture is, or certainly should be, held in universal esteem, with a side-order mantra of 'keep politics out of art!'

We also need to consider that when Hoggart and his contemporaries were addressing these newish consumer culture issues in the 1950s, there was a much closer focus on social class as the great arbiter of taste and consumption. This is no longer true as the focus of the producers and consumers has shifted focus to include issues around gender and ethnicity, misogyny and racism. What we now see increasingly is advertising re-framed to show the consumption activities of women and people of colour. To some extent this 'exposure', this visibility, and insertion in to the public consciousness does interpret and reflect significant change in everyday life, but clearly not for all. Just as culturally lead distinctions within the working classes say, in the past, was always relevant to understanding taste and consumption, or not. The overall picture is more diffuse with less certainty for observers and the observed.

In talking about commodities consumed, of any form including 'the arts', we should be aware that not everything is what it seems to be, or what we are told it is. Obviously objects appear to have a clear objective function; we need a bottle opener, so we buy and use one taking in to consideration affordability for us, and even some aesthetic considerations, who knows. And, this is where the subjective begins to play a role in both consumption and production values. Commodities also have a symbolic value, reflecting specific consumers, and the zeitgeist. Particular objects do also connote their high and low status place in everyday life and society. Indeed, in many ways given all the social interaction and communication involved in these cultural processes, they are society, and of course invariably acquire a fetish status. A must-have value that overrides all common sense; over-riding needs before wants.

As a consequence of these societal factors and changes in aspiration and opportunity to access a changing market place, it has been increasingly difficult for arts practitioners to transcend and challenge this commonality. Of course we have seen a trend where those people with a higher disposable income, and an eye for the artistic 'one-upmanship' can buy craft and 'artisan' goods of all kinds across the arts spectrum. But these practitioners have to try a lot harder to question the 'artistic' status quo, and keep one step ahead of the gift shop! This is not a new problem of course, consider William Morris chaffing over the reality of selling his desirable arts products to the 'swinish rich'. Mass production and the broadening of middle class and middle brow culture has flooded the market place. Oh joy.

There is also an element of cultural nostalgia here, which has allowed the good, the bad, and the ugly (depending on your taste) to be re-mixed via folksy renditions of what people have been persuaded to believe previous cultural lives were like. This is part of 'the invention of tradition', for example the enormous amount of money and political energy expended in the last two hundred years to create the rites and rituals centrality to British life, of

79

The Monarchy. The contemporary 'soap opera of the Monarchy, magnified by the media, gives (otherwise often sensible) people something to relate to. Dysfunctional families are regular TV fodder. It is quite clear that we live in the era of 'customised capitalism', 'if you liked and bought that, you'll love this'. We are being tracked and manipulated, living in a constant loop of immediate gratification. Vulgar and banal is the norm.

Perhaps we could live with the cleverness of contemporary capitalism set to sell us stuff at a profit, if it wasn't for the fact that most of these commodities are made by near slave labour children, and under totalitarian regimes in a global market place. And, at home, with all this freedom of choice, apparent super abundance, tens of thousands of people are living on or below the poverty line, homeless, hungry, helpless, abandoned by what is left of welfare services, denied opportunity and any hope of being offered a serious alternative to this life.

The people with money, security, opportunity and good taste can cope with the ever downward spiral of this monolithic cultural life, because they can moan about stuff, but still bask in the glow of a pop culture (the dominant culture of the day) that can still titillate them. Smugness, and self-satisfaction, is one of the worst characteristics of a pusillanimous and in the main conservative middle class. Possessive individualism feeding on the relative privileges of a broken society.

Music is also a good example here; it really does matter to some people that a Beethoven sonata should be played on a 'piano' contemporary to the man himself; although later in his life he could not hear the end result anyway. In general terms the Heritage Industry, now a key consciousness raising and profit making part of the Cultural Industries in general, has a lot to answer for. Occasionally 'searching the cultural archive' can have beneficial effects, for example, the 're-discovery' of many 'artists' consistently ignored because of their class, gender or ethnicity.

Throughout this essay I will return to arguments about tradition, heritage and the creative industries. What constitutes 'Heritage'? What are the criteria for 'anything' to be deemed to be of our heritage has become both vague, and ubiquitous. Whose heritage are we talking about? 'Our' heritage, our cultural past, or, one imposed by someone in the 'dream and aspiration factory. Which, as already suggested, usually ends up being a set of easily to hand clichés, freezing of history. A good example of this very much in the present public consciousness, are statues. What we have seen recently is an oppositional movement to question the appropriateness of having public statues of slave traders, or imperialists on horseback. These aspects of visual culture are, often by the very nature of tradition/heritage, taken for granted, that frozen history which does however often represent an acceptance with the maintenance of the status quo. Recent actions would suggest that this no longer the case. Some people say that some statues, like Colston in Bristol, would be better off in a museum, a relic not quite confined to the 'dustbin of history, but certainly re-contextualised with a different narrative of role and value. Who has the power to make these decisions about what value we place on this or that cultural object is being challenged, narratives contested.

It is also clear that with the consumption of cultural artefacts we are dealing here with 'transitional objects', something that a person(s) uses to move them psychologically from one condition of being to another, or for whom 'that' object has some special resonance. How long did it take you to give up that favourite teddy bear? So, of course people invest meaning in to objects, but who produces, sells, promotes and sanctions that object. Who has cultural agency here?

What we also have here is a continuous history of deep cultural traditions of the four countries that make up the UK. Or, one might add, the un-united kingdom, because of the centuries old desire of these separate peoples to do their own thing. In England, even allowing for the log time historical divisions between north and south, there is constant desire to return to the cultural identity of 'Old England'. Or even a 'Folk England'. Throughout the

81

nineteenth century there are successive, but often complementary cultural movements, for example Arts & Crafts that want to assert a traditional Englishness, a vernacular, that values and promotes a heritage worth celebrating. Musicians like Vaughan Williams and his friend and collaborator Gustav Holst, both brought up in Gloucestershire, mined this 'Old England' culture for their musical idiom.

What we do know is that the purpose, the everyday role of art, was discussed in antiquity and has never stopped being high on the agenda of discussions about 'what is art?'. A recurrent theme over all this time has been that art exists to help bring order to human experience; to describe those lives and place them in to some meaningful form, a form that then manifests itself in to a culturally recognisable and understandable 'thing'; a picture, music, song, literature and so on. Of course as a Sociologist I would argue that these creative, created, outcomes are contextualised by time and locality. But, also by our conscious selves.

In our post-Freud world (but a long life to his ideas) we have become used to the argument that a good deal of our beliefs and behaviour are dictated by our unconscious drivers and desires. These desires are then manifested in many ways including our creative outputs; painting a picture, writing music, film/illusion/fantasy, and so on. But also by entering in to the goods, services and cultural market places to consume some 'thing' in order to satisfy this desire, need and want. It is clear that the Twentieth century was a significant time for the expansion of the means of communication, especially so with greater literacy mixed with a modicum of education, all enhanced, even exaggerated by, the range of new telecommunications technologies that brought us static and moving images, radio and television etcetera.

Freud, like other theorists in the Modern era, dominated as it has been by industrial and finance capitalism, argued that living in the modern world 'could' render us neurotic (social pathology in everyday life); so are we all neurotic. The key issue is how neurotic are we, and do we have control over

82

it? Does it make any difference to any person, artist or not, that we are aware of our neurosis and the (artistic) consequences of this? Do we need to have therapy to understand ourselves and unlock the true creative self? Does an artistic sensibility, and practice, help us to deal with this dimension of our everyday lives? This was certainly a key issue for surrealists, who get a further mention later in this essay, and I will return to this issue in general, but it has to be addressed because theories about the role of the individual and collective unconscious mind has been significant.

On the question of theory, of which there is plenty cited and used in this essay, I should emphasise again that for me theory is more of a verb than a noun. Theorising is an active dimension to our lives, especially so amongst that large section of the population who do not claim that they are doing it on a daily basis. In the world of academia, certainly in Sociology, Theory is everywhere. As Eric Hobsbawm has argued about the French; 'every fashion requires a theory'! (1994) And, we also know that fashions on theory change, there are 'paradigm shifts', i.e. one dominant set of rules for practice replaced or superseded, by another set of rules for people to adopt as their frame of reference, their 'guiding light'. In the last few decades it is clear that throughout the academic world no one body of theory has been totally dominant; there are always many challengers for the monopoly of truth. If the legitimacy is challenged and seen to be wanting, power is then seen as contestable, and certain conventional ideas/theories about authority is weekend.

In various parts of this essay I emphasise the doing, putting into practice (praxis), and reflecting upon the outcomes of that theoretical action. I have mentioned my use of Critical Theory, which put simply means using theory and knowledge development to describe everyday life with a focus on the uneven distribution of power. A good deal of what I argue in this essay about culture and cultural artefacts, concerns the use and abuse of power. Critical Theorists challenge the status quo that maintains these inequalities, and which then reinforces the idea that this situation is normal and acceptable. From this challenge we see many more people claiming their own cultural agency. This has been very evident in our recent increasingly multi-cultural years Their voice is increasingly heard, especially so through artistic creativity in many ways.

As a constant part of my dual practice; theorist/writer and teacher/talker; I sought to incorporate these issues in to the curriculum that I designed and delivered. For example, 'Community and Culture', a study of the concepts, theories and empirical studies of Community and Culture in modern Britain. Community has been worked on a lot by Sociologists, but Culture much less so, and as an attempt to explore the inter-relationship between the two, very rarely. I also offered a course on Popular Culture, which while still considering theory and case studies, encouraged students to explore a much more specific area of their interest, and tended to see students developing their researching skills in a local setting.

And as cited elsewhere, I later drew on this design and delivery work when asked in 1997 to create a degree course pathway 'Cultural Interpretation and Practice'. A key aim of this course was to introduce students to theories of culture, and contextual issues along the lines of those discussed in this essay, but essentially to encourage students to bring together 'theory' with action, i.e. their emerging practice in 'the arts' in the widest sense of that term. So, a work in progress praxis which I hoped with clarify for them an identity to aid shaping their practice. I had already in the 1970s-90s, designed and taught similar courses tailored more specifically for my Oxford students, looking at the connections between community, culture, the media and popular music.

With all these concerns in mind, let us return to the key ideas of ideology and hegemony, and explore the meanings and usage of these concepts. Do they help us to understand what is going on in our lives now and in the future, and why this is happening? Anyone who points to the detrimental effects of the media and other culture industries must justify their claim.

Hegemony

This in turn brings me to hegemony. As with ideology, it is not my intention to provide an extensive discussion of this concept, rather my aim is to demonstrate why it has been of use to me. Essentially, hegemony is about both domination and leadership. Hegemonism as a concept was used by the likes of Mao Tse-tung to describe a cultural version of imperialism. This is much in the same way that many writers have suggested that working class (creative) cultures have been 'colonised' by the dominant economic class; hijacked, repackaged, glamorised, and sold back to the very same people at a profit. This version of hegemony suggests that the ruling class/elites in any society have maintained their ownership and control of the cultural apparatuses. This sense of culture would be broad enough to encompass schooling, means of information exchange, control of the 'air-waves', and so on, as well as the media and other standard culture industries. In short, belief systems that are an integral part of people's everyday lives and values. This use of hegemony suggests that the very manner in how most people gather and exchange information and knowledge (even about themselves) is managed and orchestrated by those with vast amounts of power and control over our everyday lives. These processes are deliberate and exploitative, actively seeking to maintain and develop a complex set of structures that directly reproduce the oppression of the many by the few. But, in order to do this the capture of 'hearts and minds' of people is essential.

Or to put this a slightly different way, here is Stuart Hall (1977) quoted in Hebdige (1989);

'The term hegemony refers to a situation in which a provisional alliance of certain social groups can exert "total social authority" over other subordinate groups, not simply by coercion or by the direct imposition of ruling ideas, but by "winning and shaping consent so that the power of the dominant classes appear both legitimate and natural". Hegemony can only be maintained so long as the dominant classes "succeed in framing all competing definitions within their range" so that subordinate groups are, if not controlled, then at least contained within an ideological space which does not seem at all "ideological": which appears instead to be permanent and "natural", to lie outside history, to be beyond particular interests'.

So once again, who says what to whom and in what conditions, plus to remind ourselves that we all take cultural and creative action but not necessarily in conditions of own choosing. Hence my insistence throughout this essay for a focus on the conditions of practice for all artists.

The issue of everyday discourse is often cited by Sociologists as a key aspect of these processes. And to add to the above; who says what to whom, for what purposes, and with what outcomes? The idea of vocabularies of motive alert us to questions about the available language for people to express themselves in all aspects of their everyday lives. Obviously, we are all likely to use different aspects of 'our' language for different occasions and purposes, for example the words, the idioms, that we use in formal discourse, at work say, or school, is probably different from usage in our leisure time, in family settings, or friendship groups and so on. Of course we do have some agency in what we say, how we say it, and to whom for whatever reasons. These forms of language are embedded in our culture groups and membership of those social formations. We are always adopting and adapting. But, we are likely to be bounded by what are the dominant forms of discourse. As I have discussed elsewhere in this essay, how self-conscious we are of these processes is a different matter, and I would argue that the spread of literacy has and does make a difference. Educational experience can make a difference to how we see the world, formulate what we consider to be appropriate questions, put needs and concerns on agendas, and seek the agency that could challenge the status quo of the relations of power that we are all a part of.

We can, for example, see that some (self-identified) cultural groups insist on speaking their own language as a key aspect to asserting their identity. I make

86

mention of this in my comments on Nationalism.

Through the manipulation of culture and politics those with power do not always have to resort to armed means to protect and promote their privileges. So, politics is not enough, the cultural, and belief system modes in general, these heights of power must be conquered and transformed through a renewed democratic practice. Based on past and current experience, this would require a socialised economy, what some people would call socialism, which being an 'ism' is of course about ideas. And in turn ideas alone are not enough, action and dedicated practice must follow. First and fore-most this would be social and democratic; fairness and cooperation must our daily 'bread and butter'. The constant struggle for democratic cultural values.

It follows therefore that a second sense of hegemony has derived largely from Lenin, and, importantly, from Gramsci, in the early twentieth century. This sense of the concept emphasises the need for the intellectual, cultural and political forces of opposition to combine in challenging the 'cultural' dominance of the 'ruling/controlling class' whoever that might be, country by country, but increasingly globally. This system of alliances works out a strategy of opposition, and deploys the means whereby the regular duping of the people can be challenged and stopped. The nefarious activities of these rulers and controllers must be exposed for what they are: privileged, selfish, greedy, short-sighted, and so on. As I suggest above, cultural action is required. In his book 'Common Culture' Willis says;

'A central theme of this book has been how symbolic resources are mobilized through grounded aesthetics for the construction of meaning and identity – a pursuit of a kind of wholeness…The wholeness of belonging to larger traditional structures of value, feeling and identity becomes less possible and yet the contradictions and terrible fissures of daily life continue in need of desperate repair.' (Willis 1990 p.158)

And yes, Willis was writing in 1990, and here we are in 2023, post Blair

(Thatcher in trousers) et al, and has anything changed for the better? I think not. As Willis goes on to say the 'repair' that was desperately needed then was still in the hands of market forces, still 'colonising' most cultural forces and resources. What we experience today is an updated, and even more glitzy version of the power holding and money making set of values, and actions, that Willis was discussing thirty-three years ago!

Of course there are some green shoots of cultural independence, and many individuals and collectives are aspiring to gain cultural agency. The growth in awareness for the absolute necessity for more grass-roots control over cultural resources, and the demand for a more imaginative and inclusive role for cultural policy of all kinds.

It will become clear to the reader that the main reason for my embarking on this very personal essay is to both record my own cultural practice, my actions in writing and talking to emphasise my commitment to the continuous inter-relation of theory and practice. I have commented in this essay on my recent, and on-going cultural practice where I live, helping to develop an arts and culture strategy, helping to build an infrastructure of and for arts practitioners, editing a weekly column (the community education column) in my local commercial newspaper, and working with local enthusiasts to 'put things on'. I take my impresario role very seriously.

A crucial element of a challenge to oppressors is the goal of a genuine democratic socialism: bringing together the common ownership of the wealth-creating resources in society, through the processes of inclusive decision- making; and returning the collective ownership of labour to people; with means of discussing the appropriate ways in which human labour can be used to meet the needs of all.

So, the aim of this brief excursion into theory is to demonstrate why the struggle for democratic cultural values is a struggle - and why we need to engage in that challenge together.

A further related aspect to these contexts is for me to explain what I mean by democratic values, and democratic cultural values.

First and foremost, democratic values are those that put democratic relations at the top of our social agendas. Of course there remains a diverse range of definitions of democracy, could it realistically be otherwise? Many people feel that the goal of a true democracy is this: a multi-party representative parliamentary system, with a fully enfranchised population, within certain agreed guidelines, one person one vote, with choice. This fits with the 'liberal democracy' of most modern societies. However, the former Soviet Union was a good example of where some people claimed that in a one-party state most of the criteria above still applied. There have been other variations on these themes, which I leave the reader to explore. One of the recent issues in Britain has been around the actual role and influence of opposition parties. Since the election of Blair & Co. in 1997, it has been argued that, given New Labour's majority, and the weakness of the other political parties, we did in effect live in a one-party State. This line of argument does not only raise questions about the opposition parties, it also focuses attention on the nature and role of the Parliamentary Labour Party (PLP). How effective is the PLP in regulating and trimming the activities of the Executive? Does the role of backbenchers in Parliament on select committees give us cause for hope? Are most of the PLP merely 'lobby fodder'? And, if they are, is this because as professional politicians they are all desperate to keep their jobs and careers? Most of the 'old guard' in the PLP have tended to become members of the 'awkward squad' that regularly 'sounds-off' about the excesses of Blair, Brown & Co. This is also true for most other political parties in the UK since 2010.

This can make for temporary entertainment, but we should remember that most of these 'Old Labour' stalwarts were on the right of the Labour Party, and actively involved in the various witch-hunts to expose and expel any left-wing and Marxist members. This task, having been completed under Kinnock's watch, left the field clear for the rag, tag and bobtail of the SDP, Tory defectors, and neo-liberals like Blair and Mandelson, to move in and take over unopposed. As Tony Benn often pointed out the dominant tendency in the PLP has been social democratic (at best) and not democratic socialist. As I have discussed above, the former were always happy to enter in to deals with the capitalist class around State funding and compensatory welfare, believing, as they did, and do, that concessions can be wrung from the privileged and powerful. Management of the State apparatus by such governments invariably plays into the hands, and does the daily bidding of the real ruling class.

Democratic socialists have generally argued that without the social ownership of the economy, and the wholesale empowerment of all people through a genuinely representative system of decision-making in society, there will be no fundamental change in inequality and injustice, or in actual government.

As I have discussed earlier, it is clear that the culture industries in general, and the media in particular, play a crucial role in the maintenance of a society where inequality, injustice, and privilege are reproduced on a daily basis. The media tends to represent, and reproduce dominant values that serve to maintain the status quo of unequal power relations in our everyday lives. The media influence, of course is not all one-way-traffic, and people of diverse cultural kinds place a range of meanings on their lives, and the world around them. However, the dominance of consumer capitalism, neo-liberal rhetoric on individualism and choice, and the real lack of access that most people have to decision-making, is anti-pathetic to an active democracy. Indeed, the current crisis of disengagement from the conventional political processes, and a pervasive sense of disenfranchisement among many people, has yet again thrown the State 'managers' in to a panic. We are once again witnessing a flurry of activity around 'active citizenship', and 'community spirit regeneration'. The Pandemic years highlighted this situation.

90

The Arts, national values, and education

Any discussion about ideology in general and specific ideologies in particular, will eventually touch on Nationalism, a vast set of ideas about nationhood, identity, and struggles for change. Many histories of the struggles around nation building emphasise the key role of the arts in the development of sets of values that form the basis of national and, inevitably, the traditional and residual culture of a 'people' who hold those values most dearly. An example that comes to mind if of Jean Sibelius, the late nineteenth, early twentieth century Finish musician, whose musical tone poem Finlandia, was when written in 1899, and still is today the unofficial liberational Finish national anthem.

If we are to enter in to a discussion about national cultures, we will also soon encounter the nature and role of folk heroes and music. Many musicians of the last two hundred years have incorporated their local cultural music, 'folk' in to their own 'modernist' compositions. These nationalist struggles invariably involve nation building, and music and the other arts can do that very well; a rallying call that can, however, easily move to the bombastic values end of the artistic spectrum. Anthems being one such example. One good cause can often obliterate the claims of other minorities. There is also the problem with tradition, of which folk cultures, and cultural artefacts are regularly cited. The fact is that the notion of 'tradition' confirms that the cultural structures that for example provided actual conditions of practice, production and consumption, have outlived their time and place, the socio-historical nature of their existence, and have been resurrected for some purpose without roots. It may well be the case though that 'some' mythologised roots will be created to fill that historical gap.

We should however, be careful in our understanding of 'folk' as an explanation for certain art forms, especially music. There are a myriad of uses and explanations for what 'folk' actually means and conveys, and has the same kind of vagueness problems as 'popular culture'; who is making claims and why? A commonplace explanation for the continued enthusiasm for 'folk' is mentioned by A.L.Lloyd's contested attribution to 'The mother of folklore is poverty' (Lloyd 1967 p.11)

Of course, as I have already suggested radical, even socialist, values are associated with usage. Understandably Lloyd cites Cecil Sharp (who was a socialist, and contemporary of Vaughan William and Holst) from the previous generation of folk song hunters, who argued for the importance of a folk tradition as oppositional to the status quo of their own time. Escaping the alienation created by the rationalism of 'modern society'.

This does of course link to an abundance of evidence of the patriotic love of nation; in general, and non-specific poverty related terms; of place and people, tipping over in to an overtly flag waving jingoistic posturing. Many artists, particularly perhaps musicians, have had their patriotic and grounded aesthetic creativity misunderstood. I am just listening to Edward Elgar, a composer who often hated the many interpretations of his orchestral work, for example the addition of lyrics which he considered inappropriate.

However, this is a partial view, and many musicians have and would disagree. The 'arts for art's sake' set of values is also not confined to musicians. Aesthetes like Oscar Wilde would take issue with you. Here is Vaughn Williams on this knotty issue;

'Why do we make music? There can be no doubt that at certain emotional moments most people want to make particular kinds of noises. Indeed, we may say with Carlyle that if we search deep enough there is music everywhere. But why? Neither I, nor anyone else, has been able to solve that problem. But one thing we can be certain of: we do not compose, sing, or play music for any useful purpose…music is just music, and that is, to my mind, its great glory. How then do we justify it, it is its own justification; that is all I know and all I need to know.'

(Vaughan Williams 1955 p.205, but see bibliography)

But, as already suggested, many 'musicians' as in other arts, are determined to see a utility in what they and others say and do.

Before saying more about music and musicians I should also add that 'nationalist' poetry is a key issue. The creation of anthologies regularly throw up anomalies of national identity and the motives of editors to include or exclude. This often falls in to the convention that something labelled British, is in reality English. And, does this English include Old or Middle English? Or Latin, or…? In a response to being included in an anthology of Contemporary British Poetry, Seamus Heaney remarked that his passport was Green. Why would he, or any other poet, wish to speak in the language of their coloniser?

In my 2012 book, 'Access to Eden' about Arts & Crafts and Garden City influences on 1920s public sector housing building, I quoted Ralph Vaughan Williams from his 1934 book 'National Music and other essays';

'Music, like language, derives ultimately from its basic beginnings…About fifty years ago, Cecil Sharp made his epoch-making discovery of English folk-song. We young musicians were intoxicated by these tunes. We said to ourselves, "Here are beautiful melodies of which, until lately, we knew nothing. We must emulate Grieg and Smetana, and build up, on the basis of these tunes, a corpus of compositions arising out of our country and character." And we proceeded to pour out Overtures and Rhapsodies and Ballad Operas to show the world that we were no longer a land without music.'

This is from an essay that VW wrote in 1955, three years before his death, and sums up very briefly the life changing impact the folk idiom on their role as English musicians. VW with his good friend Holst amongst other contemporaries grasped the opportunity to reinforce the 'English-ness' of their work to counter-pose the dominance of German music in their youth. Many German music critics had characterised England as the land without (its own) music. VW's music has often been seen as Pastoral, and yes, he and others did explicitly draw on their direct experience of walking the countryside as inspiration for their work. Not unlike the contemporaneous enthusiasm for open-air painting amongst 'The Impressionists' and others. But, the compositions of VW and Holst are in fact much closer to the social realist, earthiness, of Thomas Hardy's novels.

A further aspect of both VW's and Holst's quest to create an authentic 'national' music was their sense of responsibility to recover Tudor music from the musical dustbin of history. The music of the Tudor era, notably for VW the work of Thomas Tallis had fallen into obscurity, and he was determined to incorporate those idioms in to his own work, most famously perhaps his 'Fantasia on a theme by Thomas Tallis' from 1909, first performed at the Three Choirs Festival at Gloucester.

For me there has always been something here of a quest for 'the Spirit of England', or, a la William Blake, the search for and recovery of 'Albion', the much mythologised England. Of course there has been a long tradition of writing, and painting, and music making focused on the landscape of England. This time immemorial, embedded in the land, and the sky, and the weather, sense of belonging, is a fundamental aspect of identity seeking for the English, just as it is for other peoples. Is it so surprising that Vaughan Williams' tune 'The Lark Ascending' (1914) remains so popular? Also worth recalling that VW was one of several pre-1914 musicians to set the poems from A.E.Houseman's 'A Shropshire Lad' (1896) he of 'The Blue Remembered Hills'. One of the tunes VW wrote was for 'Bredon Hill', where the poems protagonist reflects, 'and hear the larks so high'.

Lurking in the cultural background is also the 'Norman Yoke' issue. This term comes from the post 1066 oppressive nature of 'English' feudalism i.e. the Norman invaders had set out to inforce their culture upon the Anglo Saxons. The Walter Scott myth making (in 'Ivanhoe') around Robin Hood being perhaps a well- known example, along with Charles Kingsley's 'Hereward the

94

Wake'. A literary device to promote a Romantic and nostalgic view of Anglo-Saxon culture and commoners law. This idea has often reappeared in times of national turmoil, for example during the English Civil War, when Gerrard Winstanley of The Diggers faction cited The Yoke as a antecedent to Charles 1st 's Royalist anti-democracy.

Holst, like many of his late nineteenth century contemporaries were Christian Socialists, and/or deists. Holst's musical interests were genuinely global, but his formative years in Hammersmith, London, had a significant political edge. He was involved with the Hammersmith Socialists, conducted the Groups choir, knew William Morris, and went on the write an Elegy for Morris, a part of Holst's Cotswolds Suite. The utopian and millennial aspects of Morris' ideas certainly had a lasting influence on the youthful musician. VW spent his life in the borderland between Christianity and agnosticism. Considering these musicians, as with the painters, many of them Pantheists, Samuel Palmer comes to mind, and writers like Hardy, who sought to grasp the virtually ungraspable. Also, given that all of these people had a reverence for the past, that the group of artists that Palmer belonged to in the early nineteenth, took their lead from William Blake called themselves 'The Ancients'. All of these 'artists' discussed above sought agency, for themselves in their various artistic quests, and for the authentic England that they cherished in all its complexity.

And, to mention an Irishman, Jack Yeats the painter, who sought to create an art that was not the final word on 'life', but a constant question about life.

I should also add a brief note of a geographical and cultural quirk that has always pleased me. I regularly draw William Morris in to the orbit of Holst and VW, so just to mention that Cheltenham, where Holst was born, is a few miles west of Down Ampney, where VW was born, which is a few miles west of Kelmscott Manor where Morris lived. Set between them, a cultural ghost, is Cirencester the great Roman town (Corinium) established on the meeting place of the Fosse way, Ermin Way and Akeman Street. And all contained on the Ordnance Survey Landranger Map 163!

The Hungarian Bela Bartok is a well-known example of the desire to both seek out the tunes and songs of his usually rural indigenous people on the Hungarian/Romanian border, and develop those in to his own compositions. Bartok is also a good example of a musician who ignored official national boundaries, in his case for example the one between Hungary and Romania, to do his ethnomusicology.

This facet of the creative imagination covers all of the arts, not just musical cultures; the variety of dialects not the least of the issues to consider. But the crux of the matter here is to 'consider', and not accept as alternative for historical reality.

Of course these folk narratives in whatever from they take are stories, even 'autobiographies', and they may well inspire us to take actions of our own to right wrongs, even attempt to re-write our national/cultural selves, but, they are stories, they are interpretations of social life, and not a comprehensive analysis.

However, a major problem with this is that the stories we tell ourselves as nation builders are not necessarily true. The reality of 'who' we are as a people may be myth. And, as I have suggested above the arts have a lot to answer for when it comes to myth making, the telling, and crucially, re-telling of stories not just about ourselves but also about those 'others' who are not like us. It is usually the case that those actively engaged in myth making regard everyone else's stories as ideology, deliberate story telling for political reasons, but of course not their own. Who decides what a past was/is? History is written for now, todays audience, and usually by those with most power and control over the means of communication. No surprises then that many people in many culture groups, with their own sense of 'history' and values, come in to conflict, attempt to resist the dominant narrative that comes from the top down.

One important commentator here is Paul Gilroy, who with his book 'There Ain't No Black in the Union Jack' (1987) made a valuable contribution to the debates on a post-colonial life in the UK. Empire lingers, and still has an influence on the prevailing ideology of hierarchy based on ethnicity. Stuart Hall in his many contributions on resistance to the status quo for example, 'The Empire Strikes Back' (1982) not only discussed the virulent racism of the time, especially the heavy-handed police role, also emphasised the role of everyday creative cultural responses which contained a critique liberal politics.

Can the narrative of the State, whoever is in government, be trusted given the close inter-connection with the ruling elites? In his book 'Crusoe's Footsteps' (1990) Patrick Brantlinger, argued that the DIY rational world of Robinson Crusoe was shaken by discovering 'the footprint in the sand'. Paranoia set in, who was this enemy within, how should he respond to this threat to an established order? Brantlinger suggests that the Bourgeoisie in the western world have been constantly required to look over their cultural shoulder for fear of savages disrupting their ordered world.

One major contribution of Cultural Studies that I have already argued is to emphasise the necessity to adopt an anthropological perspective on everyday life in the UK and elsewhere. The nineteenth anthropologists (Ethnographers) devoted themselves to seeking out and attempting to understand the many exotic non-industrialised tribal cultures in the colonies and beyond. They assumed that the perfection of Western society and culture was the norm, the benchmark against which all other human culture should be measured. This approach to humankind was increasingly challenged in the twentieth century period of de-colonisation, where multi-culturalism became an acknowledged reality of society and everyday life. As I have argued above this situation was, and continues to be resisted by those who see the loss of Empire as a personal affront; ethnocentric values still exist in this society despite the general acceptance of a cultural diversity being of value.

It is clear that in another dimension of everyday life The Establishment as a national identity narrative that emphasises the militaristic character of our traditions as a nation; the publicly sanctified status afforded to these 'traditional' values. Consider for example the outrage in government and media circles when in 1981 Michael Foot wore a green duffle coat at the Cenotaph Remembrance day event. Breaking the established code of dress for such events may have reflected upon Foot's 'old labour' and CND credentials and values, but was considered unacceptable because it undermined the usual heavy-handed dose of hypocrisy and sentimentality.

Something similar happened many years later when Jeremy Corbin wore an 'ordinary' jacket to his first Prime Ministers questions, PMQs, in sharp contrast to the expensive formal suits worn my Cameron and co. Corbin underlined his 'non-conformity' by asking questions provided by his constituents.

Liberals, especially perhaps those associated with the arts (and therefore often well-meaning) often perpetuate the idea that the oppression of the powerful can be diluted or deflected by the creativity of the arts. Reading a novel about the poor and suffering, the marginalised and ignored, can provide us with an alternative narrative, which it does of course, but one that overrides reality?

This is why twentieth century thinkers like the historian Eric Hobsbawm kept reminding us that empathy is not a valid substitute for research based evidence and analysis. As a society we simply have to do the hard work, and not kid ourselves that seeing a good play is going to cut the mustard. (And of course as a Sociologist I am compelled to tell you that!)

The European Romantic Movement of the nineteenth century has a lot to answer for here. Right across the arts, but especially perhaps in music the most, for example Chopin, Romanticism unleashed the creative expression of emotional attachment to 'great' causes like nationalism. Through the promotion of emotional expression these arts offer up ideas and feelings about national identity, who we really are as a people. In music particularly a more rhythmic, melodic and harmonic phraseology coincided with, and reinforced, a desire for freedom, and a psychological and political commitment to change. Maybe even mounting the barricades to fight for this freedom?

But, if listening to music, or watching a play say, makes us angry enough to go away and do 'the research', we would be better off, but so in all likelihood would be the people whose needs should be met? This is commonplace in TV-land, where people watching 'Reality' shows actually believe that this is reality in all its complexity, rather than some very manipulated story telling that might (apparently) be entertaining! Watching/listening to politicians can have the same effect on the lazy minded, accept the first and easiest story that comes along approaches to understanding everyday life.

So, on the question of myth making, I want to focus some attention on the English dimension to this significant issue. I will start by reminding the reader of the of a Department of Education statement from 2014;

'We want to create and enforce a clear and rigorous expectation on all schools to promote the fundamental British values of democracy, the rule of law, individual liberty and mutual respect, and tolerance of those with different faiths and beliefs.'

Of the many contentious ideas in this statement, the word 'enforce' does leap off the page. Some people would certainly question whether such a determination to impose a certain list of values on everyone is even consistent with us being tolerant of others? The Nationalist rhetoric around this policy did come at a time of exit from the European Union!

It is also noteworthy that the State shifted responsibility for ensuring the promotion of these values from the Home Office (the ministry of the interior) to Education.

This whole issue raises questions about the ability of those with power and authority in any age to control music, for example through banning folk or oppositional music, or depriving people of their traditional musical instruments, and by constantly reinforcing by any available means what the powerful and self -proclaimed consider to be culture of high value. One of the key tasks of Cultural Studies has been to 'deconstruct' the motives and means behind this oppressive situation to offer an alternative view, and providing space for previously excluded people to offer all of us their own cultural meanings. Outsiders becoming as a right, insiders.

So, a big question for me is whether holding on to a set of values that celebrates and practices national arts, is acceptable? Why would we still wish to champion artists of all kinds because they are English, or British, or from Devon? Looking at popular arts objects over time is always an interesting barometer of taste and fashion. What music do people listen to? Why that music? Where does it originate from, does that matter? I have noted over many years the enthusiasm for having prints of well-known French 'Impressionist' painters like Monet on their walls. Why that art object rather than a contemporary 'English' painter, like Walter Sickert? This is especially interesting when we know that these people, and many contemporaries, travelled back and forth across the English Channel?

Is this a lack of arts education, media narrowness, or what is available in galleries and poster shops?

In addition to discussing 'Nationalism's some acknowledgement should be made to Localism. Living in East Devon since 1996 has been a pleasure, enhanced by my exploration of my homeland. Being a devoted Anglophile would have already been evident in what I have said above, and much of my practice over recent years has focused on my engagement with and celebration of my locality. This is one aspect of my vocabulary of motives, I am using text here to illustrate my values and a reason to practice how I do.

100

In chapter 7 I have included some articles that have been written in recent years as a part of my Community Education Column (CEC) in our local (weekly) newspaper. A good deal of my recent writing for the CEC has been linked to an involvement with Arts & Culture East Devon (ACED), a local networking group across East Devon which is now a key aspect of a new policy and practice initiative by East Devon District Council (EDDC) driven by a ten-year Culture Strategy. I have included a recent CEC article here to highlight the importance of placing significant general issues on arts and culture in to a local context, starting with 'Whose Heritage'

Whose Heritage?

I have been thinking a lot recently about tradition, heritage and the creative industries.

The Heritage Industry has expanded considerably in recent decades, and become a key aspect of the leisure and tourist offer. We have become accustomed to seeking out 'the old' and interesting, from redundant and rusting industrial plant to museums of the maritime. The National Trust remains a people's favourite, but has had to do some serious thinking in recent years about the commonplace narrative attached to grand houses and their previous occupants. There have been several TV series recently, putting families in to 'historical' situations in order for them to both struggle, cope and have their consciousness raised about life 'in the past'. Can we, should we, reproduce 'pasts' (create a simulacrum) to try out how life and culture was, to help inform and educate, as well as with the TV stuff, entertain? Is there scope here to enliven the school based History curriculum for the benefit of children? I went to school in Southampton which has a very well preserved medieval town, by the sea of course. A lot of what is left is Tudor, and resonates with cross-channel trade (and wars). When our time came to discuss the Tudors at school I recall asking if we were going to do a field trip to the 'old town'. The suggestion was met with a swift rebuke!

As the pages of The Exmouth Journal demonstrate, many people do care a good deal about having an authentic 'reading' of our past. Music is a good example here; it really does matter to some people that a Beethoven sonata should be played on a 'piano' contemporary to the man himself; although later in his life he could not hear the end result anyway. In general terms the Heritage Industry, now a key consciousness raising and profit making part of the Cultural Industries in general, has a lot to answer for. Occasionally 'searching the cultural archive' can have beneficial effects. For example, the 're-discovery' of many 'artists' consistently ignored because of their class, gender or ethnicity.

What constitutes 'Heritage'? What are the criteria for any cultural artifact to be deemed to be of our heritage has become both vague, and ubiquitous. Whose heritage are we talking about? Our heritage, our cultural past, or, one imposed by someone in the 'dream and aspiration factory'? Which in turn usually ends up being a set of easily-to-hand clichés; 'freezing' history. Statues are a good example of current public consciousness. What we have seen recently is an oppositional movement to question the appropriateness of having public (place) statues of slave traders, or imperialists on horseback, and so on. Statues are aspects of visual culture, and often by the very nature of tradition, taken for granted. That frozen history already mentioned, does usually imply we are okay with the maintenance of the status quo socially and culturally. Recent actions would suggest that this no longer the case. Some people say that some statues, like Colston in Bristol, would be better off in a museum, a relic not quite confined to the 'dustbin of history', but certainly re-contextualised with a different narrative of role and value.

These issues are with us now as more and more cultural groups wish to assert their right to an identity with which they are comfortable. But, also more people are keen to adjust conventional, even traditional, perceptions and understandings of who they are. This demand for re-assessment of people, and their heritage, their past, is a question of value. What and who do we value, or not, and why?

In general terms, Art in all its diversity can be a place to open up these questions, to reflect upon, and re-consider what we think we know about the human condition, about people's lives and loves, as well as their frustrations and disappointments.

What I would add now to this newspaper article are some additional questions about aesthetics and utility. I have already touched on this key issue in this essay, but it is worth re-visiting this here. There is always a tension in the arts between 'arts for art's sake' and a utilitarian approach, a job to do, as a major aspect of art's function in society. Artists of all kinds have to live; food comes before philosophy, even the pursuit of the sublime; and therefore they must exist in the market place. This is certainly part of the challenge of cultural consumerism that, for example, is a day-to-day issue for artists living and working in East Devon. A way of life is also a way of living. One of the key aims of the EDDC Culture Strategy, and a driving force for all of us in ACED is to meet artistic practitioners' needs. This may be using our network to link up practitioners in a self-help mode, sharing information and ideas, or offering courses in marketing, fundraising and so on. There is a definite nature/nurture aspect to these interventions. The educational dimension to what we all do must be a constant feature of how we work.

As I have argued before, we all make and take actions, but not necessarily in conditions of our own choosing. Focusing on the conditions of practice issue is in the forefront of our minds.

'Art to order', for example for locals and tourists in East Devon, is a realistic prospect for many practitioners, but also for the many ancillary traders in the wider local economy. Maintaining these many tensions requires both an experimental and experiential approach, enhancing the unique local creative culture that makes for our locality.

TALKING

Some time ago I gave a copy of my book on Music and Everyday Life to an acquaintance, who had not read anything of mine before. Later I asked if he enjoyed the book, to which he replied that reading the text was just like my talking to him. I am still deciding whether I should be pleased with that or not?

Human beings are talkers, but are we any good at it? In fact, how much effort do we make in considering how we talk and for what purposes? Indeed, Clifford Geertz the American Anthropologist suggested that Culture is simply the ensemble of stories we tell ourselves about ourselves, an idea that features a lot in this essay. Indeed, it has often been argued that what the 'creation' of Cultural Studies has done is to enable a set of discursive practices; asked questions in the usual Critical Theory manner, and invited, even insisted upon, a discussion.

It is certainly true that there is great complexity in talking in appropriate ways depending on who we are talking to and about what.

Noam Chomsky, the American linguist argues that language is an expression of our creativity, what humans do, and has developed competence and performance dimensions to these actions. Another American (Canadian), Erving Goffman spent most of his career writing about verbal and non-verbal human and social interactions, for example in his 1967 book 'Interaction Ritual'.

Clearly we learn how to talk within our immediate social milieu, which has often been called socialisation; learning the rules of everyday life and social interaction. But this is not a one-way process, because we are constantly adopting and adapting. As I have said many times before the culture group of which we are initially a member has a profound affect on us, for example accent and vocabulary. They effect of this can make our particular life easier and more difficult. Some social and cultural theorists refer to Ethnomethodology as the process of the making and daily use of ways of life of particular cultural groups; the ways in which they have come to organise, manage their lives and deal with other people to the best of their experience and learnt ability. (For much more on this see Erickson and Cicourel listed in my bibliography).

One key issue for someone like myself is the manner in which I have transmitted ideas and information to other people, colleagues, students and a reading public. My verbal and non-verbal skills are a key issue here if I am to make what I say of any value or utility to the listeners and readers. What did he say? I have always given much thought to these issues (although some people may feel that has not helped much!). A great deal of academic life has comprised of one person taking control of the manner, flow and style, of that social interaction. The traditional academic lecture is one of the most arbitrary forms of talk devised; it can be invigorating and entertaining (see my earlier comments on this) but all too often is a waste of everyone's time. As was once said, lot of information passed from one person to others with nobody paying much attention. This serves to emphasise the routines of certain culturally determined ways of talking; and by definition listening; and the exercise of power. Someone talks to other people in the way they do because they can, feels entitled to do that, and believes it is appropriate, even legitimate. Many of the listeners may also believe these actions are legitimate, and if they do not will have to take some action. I recall that most of the undergraduate lectures I attending were very boring and virtually irrelevant to my needs. With my fellow sufferers we devised a rota to share out attendance and essential notetaking. Much better to work in the library! Over the course of my career as a teacher of Sociology I have kept my reflexive educationalist hat on, discussing with colleagues and students how best to transmit and discuss relevant bodies of knowledge, both old and new.

See my book 'Thinking about the Curriculum' (2022)

Yet again, who says what to whom, in what contexts and why?

Enter Rhetoric, the art of effective and/or persuasive speaking, especially the exploitation of figures of speech and other compositional techniques. Rhetoric was a keystone skill in the traditional Grammar school curriculum.

Many Sociologists interested in the social interactive nature of our everyday lives have concerned themselves with talking as a key aspect of any culture. I have included a piece here that draws on Goffman. Many other twentieth century social theorists have also cited rhetoric as a key issue, for example Michel de Certeau, in his best known study, 'The Practice of Everyday Life' (1984). He emphasises the disparity of power to be found in modern life between those who produce what we less powerful people consume. Another example of what C.Wright Mills called 'a vocabulary of motives', and as I have already suggested, who says what to whom, for what purposes, and in conditions often dictated so by 'the producers'. Not surprisingly these issues also concern those involved with Communications and Media Theory, so the breadth of interest in these core arguments gets bigger the more anyone looks at it.

In the 1960s the French cultural critic Roland Barthes discussed 'the rhetoric of the image', an attempt to emphasise the way our use of language in a world replete with symbols, like advertisements, have a lot to say for themselves. Bringing meaning to our awareness of symbols to such an extent that we take for granted this whole aspect of our everyday lives. Not so the 'hidden persuaders', whose purpose is very self-conscious.

While in this vein of thought I should mention Guy Debord, another influential French 'philosopher' (1932-94) who was a much more explicitly political theorist of the everyday. He is most known for his 1967 book 'The Society of the Spectacle' where he articulated that which fell within his work with the Situationist International who sought to emphasise the decline of capitalist 'civilisation' to mere surface. The truth of life had been superseded my representations of life, everyday life as a spectacle, amusing ourselves to death! Debord and his associates also argued that people need to understand their situation, and see through it to liberate themselves from the mundane and the daily reinforcement of the status quo of powerlessness. Like many theorists of the twentieth century (especially French ones), creativity and the humanity of labour and making could become a transformational practice. So, an end to theory as an abstract dead end but instead a platform for action. This dialectical process is usually referred to as Praxis; creating, making, through political consciousness a new truth, and a new civilisation.

Debord's book, and his other work certainly contributed to the Paris uprisings in May 1968, and raised political consciousness and action across Europe and the USA. Debord's ideas gelled with other highly influential writers of the time, for example Herbert Marcuse, whose 1964 book 'One Dimensional Man' offered a critique of a contemporary life of media led 'brainwashing' amongst other consumer culture ills, to keep people 'in their place'. Bread and Circuses.

So, a great deal of emphasis was placed at this time on the nature of civilisation, drawing on a very wide range of arguments, looking back to William Morris in the late nineteenth century, who in turn argued that a cultural and political transformation was essential to create a civilisation worthy of the name.

Being civilised, or 'cultured' has often rested upon the idea of proper and appropriate talking. No surprise then that the rise of Grammar schools devoted so much time to rhetoric. Shakespeare in his Grammar school would have known about this. And, in turn of course the Grammar school system drew heavily on The Classics, especially so the thinkers and writers of ancient Greece. Of these influential 'philosophers' Aristotle is usually seen as the most significant contributor to setting out the guidelines and rules for rhetoric. I will not go in to any detail here of his many categories of rhetoric (these can be looked at by any interested reader), but logic was certainly high on his list of essential aspects of 'proper' talking.

Whether a Grammar school education enabled the much mythologised man Shakespeare to write the plays now credited to 'him' is another matter. There is no necessary connection between his education that adds up to the extensive and direct experience of where many of the plays were set, or the complexity of personal moral issues expressed in the plays is another matter!

There have been hundreds of years of discussion, even talking about talking, within the study of language in general, but as with many aspects of everyday human behaviour the systematic enquiry in to everyday life started with Aristotle and his contemporaries. The unexamined life is not worth living, or so it has been asserted.

As an example of the issue raised above included here is the transcript 0f a talk from 1986,

Talk given at conference held in Oxford on 'Teaching Sociology' – taken from the book of conference papers edited by K.LAMBE & M. JOSEPH, Oxford 1986

THE SOCIOLOGY TEACHER AS ENTERTAINER

by
John Astley of Oxford Polytechnic

I was talking to a friend of mine the other day who's just come back from Los Angeles, he is a social psychologist; of course they're always going to Los An-geles; and while he was there he was talking to an American woman who has being doing research into the effects of lectures on students. She has done quite a comprehensive analysis of their response to lectures and she had come up with the information which he had passed on to me, that she had discovered that the average student spent 60% of their time in lectures daydreaming, and that of that 60%, 60% of the time was spent in sexual fantasizing. So I came to the conclusion that it doesn't really matter what I say to you this afternoon, you're probably going to have a good time. There you are, I've made you laugh already, and that may well be a part of what I want to say. Before I get down to the nitty gritty of it, and to a certain extent, I have already signalled some of my intentions of this by the very title itself, it has to be said that I'm not only suggesting that the teacher of sociology should approach his or her task in an entertaining way, I'm arguing that we, as sociologists might understand the role of teacher more clearly, if we see it, or if we understand it in terms of the role of entertaining, or what the role of the entertainer might be or agreed to be. I am taking, to a certain extent, a leaf out of other sociologists' book, particularly Goffman, in that it may help us to understand the role of teacher if we make a comparison with another role with which we are culturally familiar. There was a certain amount of discussion this morning about the teaching of teachers and so on, so that might be appropriate in any discussion we may have about the teacher role(s) we adopt or develop.

Perhaps I could just read you (it's very brief) the outline which I sent to Keith Lambe initially, because it identifies some of the issues which I think are im-portant.

'All the world is a stage' may have increasingly been reduced to the status of a cliché, but I feel the maxim still embodies a good deal of what is vital and problematic for sociologists and their attempts to put forward sociological ex-planations. My enduring interest in Erving Goffman (who on a visit to London once, I very nearly met) has required me to admit the central set of contradic-tions that face the sociologist, and sociologists who choose to teach. Goffman's concern with the culture and language of sociology, his interest in the presenta-tion of self-issue, has always made me aware that the contextual frame, the in-teraction ritual, within which the teaching of sociology might and does go on, is problematic to say the least.

Students of all kinds come to sociology, with to say the least, a fascinating mixture of attitudes and opinions about the subject. (Not to mention the subject matter). Any prospective teacher of sociology who does not acknowledge at the outset that he or she is essentially part of this subject really misses the point. How is the sociologist's presentation going to affect the student - what effect is the teacher planning to make? Part of my concern with presentation, is just how self-conscious is, or should be, the sociologist as entertainer. It is self-evident that teachers of sociology are impresarios, they are 'putters-on' of things, but classroom strategies for the sociologist should go beyond this. How much do these teachers rely on a rigid script, how much do they extemporise, what allowance is made for spontaneity, how do they use their lexicon of so-ciological knowledge, expertise and imagination in the day to day interactions that comprise their classes or lectures? It is true that these issues may be present in pedagogy in general, but it is my wish in this paper, to tease out these con-cerns, in particular in relation to sociology and sociologists.

I would add, of course, a la Goffman, that this day, this particular talk, like the others, is very much a celebrative occasion. We are engaging in a form of talk here, as are indeed our lectures and classes, which besides anything else of course, substantiates our very existence. It reaffirms again and again that we feel we have something important to say. Whether the students feel we have something important to say is very much part of the problem. I am certainly concerned with what has emerged this morning, namely the problems with dif-ferences between the meaning of the discourse, and the mechanics of the dis-course. That is an important issue for us because it does involve us in what I would call production shifts in terms of actually how we operate in the class-room, and how we move from one thing to another. Right at the beginning of "Forms of Talk" Goffman ends his preface with something which perhaps I could use here. He says "In what follows, then, I make no large literary claim, that social life is but a stage, only a small technical one that deeply incorpo-rated into the nature of talk, are the fundamental requirements of theatricality". That is really where I would start, if you like, in terms of my idea about the sociology teacher as entertainer.

Entertainment, according to the dictionary, is to occupy agreeably, amuse, re-ceive as guest, show hospitality to, admit to consideration, harbour or cherish Idea, opinion or proposal, etc. Entertain is hospitable reception, amusement, public performance. Entertainer, which is what we are talking about now, is one who gives a public entertainment. Now you may say, well it is pretty broad, but in all respects it applies to us, because indeed, we are engaged in those activities; even if we were to take as a definition of our role the business about 'show hospitality to', 'admit to consideration', 'cherish ideas', 'opinions or proposals', etc. Enough has already been said this morning in the kind of broad discussion, to show that we do feel it is relevant for us to go on engaging in, in fact even managing the framework of interactions, whereby we try and bring sociology to people, whether they feel they want it or not. Indeed, I think most of us, would by definition believe that sociology is so important that it must be good for people to be engaged in it. How effectively we transmit that to other people is, of course, a very important matter. I'm not of course suggesting that we necessarily engage in song and dance acts and so on, or that we have a very large repertoire of jokes; I do, despite what may seem apparent, take this busi-ness quite seriously. We do have again, as may have appeared this morning, we do have problems with the privileged nature of our sociological knowledge, and I think we do have

111

to be self-conscious about that. Who would admit to relishing the relative ease of resting in the lee of our privileged sociological knowledge, before once again setting course for a good buffeting on the high seas of teaching.

I think it is easy for us to hide behind our privileged sociological knowledge. It is much more difficult when we admit that it is much more problematic than it may appear to the people who are receiving this privileged knowledge from us.

I see sociological knowledge as a lexicon. We can use this lexicon of socio-logical knowledge at our disposal, say, as we might look at any painter's work. It is not just the idiosyncratic nature of the selection of this colour or that shape, but also their juxtaposition, and overall effect on our senses and sensibil-ities that makes it distinctive, that makes it stand out, that makes it important and significant. From a sociologists viewpoint this can, and should turn the or-dinary business of transmitting bodies of knowledge into something far more interesting and significant; an educational experience for the participants. Ef-fect, of course, is a vexed question in education, let alone sociology, and yes, some of the entertainment is epiphenomena. However, if well ordered the ex-perience for the participants will go beyond this and make an important contri-bution to the education of these persons, and again, once or twice this morning, I noticed in the discussion we did move very slowly towards the idea that somehow sociology might be good for a person's education. Again, that has al-ways been important to me, and the way in which we adopt our role, I think, is important there.

At this particular point, I should like to read you very briefly, a couple of ex-tracts from Erving Goffman's "Forms of Talk". All of these extracts are in fact from the chapter, 'On the lecture'. This of course for those of you who haven't seen it, is a piece of typical Goffman, extremely serious on the one hand, but to a certain extent a tongue in cheek, and self-deprecating on the other hand be-cause of course, it is a text of a lecture he gave on lectures.

He says "So the person who delivers a talk can meld himself into the occasion, by how, as a speaker, he extemporaneously or apparently extemporaneously embellishes his text using his text as a basis for a situationally sensitive rendition, mingling the living and the read, and in consequence of the way he handles himself, he can render his subject matter something that his listeners feel they can handle...but a deeper understanding is to be drawn, an understanding that speaks to the ultimate claims that society makes upon a person who performs. What the audience will sense in an esteemed speaker, as intelligence, wit and charm, what the audience will impute to him as his own internally encom-passed character; all this turns out to be generated through what he does to ef-fectively put himself at the disposal of an occasion, and hence its participants, opening himself up to it and to them, counting the rest of himself as something to be subordinated for the purpose'. (Goffman, 1981).

Again that's very self-consciously looking at the way in which we actually have to perform, the fact that we do have bodies of knowledge which we want to transmit during the course of a particular lecture, class or seminar. What I'm arguing, is that the nature of self-consciousness in terms of how we are actually going to make ourselves part of that event is very important, and I would argue that we do not think enough about it.

The speaker will have reviewed some of his remarks beforehand and may even have inscribed in them his reading copy in note form as a reminder of the foot-ing to be employed in delivering them. In all this, observed lectures are like stories or jokes - a teller can, and is encouraged to, throw himself into his tell-ing as if this telling were occurring for the first and only time.

We've all done that haven't we? The only constraint is that one of the audience may already have heard his performance, and in fact every communication fos-ters a little of this first and only illusion.

I was talking to somebody the other day who had been on a summer school at a University in the north and I asked "how was it" and they said, 'Oh, it

113

was quite good" and I said "Who did you enjoy the most?" and this person said "So and so's talk was absolutely wonderful" and I said "What was the title of his talk" and this person said "Blah Blah" and so I said "Oh yes, did he tell you the joke about, and did he put in the anecdote about, and so on" and of course by the end of this, this person realised that what the speaker had done, being a great entertainer, was to replicate what he had done before. What he does on many other occasions, and what I suspect, if we admitted it, a number of us have done as well is to appear to be offering a unique talk. He was able; be-cause of his self-consciousness in terms of how he sees himself in the role of entertainer; even though the bodies of knowledge he is transmitting are very important and significant; to make people quite easily believe that this was al-most an extemporaneous talk, or it could fall into the category of what Goffman calls "fresh talk". That is what I am doing now except in fact I am not doing "fresh talk" now, because I had already decided, that I was going to say this to you. So, this may look as if it is an aside, but of course, it's not an unplanned aside because it's actually part of my plan of what I was going to say. The main text is 'over there', I am making an explanatory remark which suggests a slightly realised version of that 'text' or 'action'.

We engage in this constantly in our classrooms even in what may look like a formal lecture, in fact what I suspect we do is to decide that we will, at various times, for example, appear to 'step down' from our text - there it is in front of us - and make an aside or make an extemporaneous point, or even have a plant in the audience who is going to raise some issue or other whereby we can ap-parently then be spontaneous, (this goes back to Goffman's point about this in-dicates our intelligence, charm, wit and spontaneity etc.,). What we are doing is using this in order to create, to manage the interaction that is taking place be-tween us and the audience.

There is an irony here. There are moments in a lecture when the speaker seems most alive to the ambience of the occasion and is particularly ready with wit and extemporaneous response to show how fully he has mobilised his spirit and mind for the moment at hand. Yet these inspired moments will often be ones to be most suspect of for during them the speaker is quite likely to be delivering something he has memorised, having happened upon an utterance that fits so well that he cannot resist re-using it in that particular slot when he gives the talk in question.

At this moment of obvious relevance, it is rarely appreciated that anecdotes are specialised for aptness, as with pat comebacks, standard excuses and other uni-versal joints of discourse, relevance is to be found not so much in the situation, as in the intrinsic organisation of the anecdote itself. The little narratives we allow ourselves to interject in a current talk, we are likely to have interjected in other talks too, let alone other presentations of the current one.

I see this as part of our whole question about sociological strategies. Certainly I would even go so far as to say it's part of how I see sociology as a wholeness, that in engaging in sociology, in trying to get our students to engage in it with us; no matter what backgrounds they may come from etc. We are managing the interaction of our classrooms, seminars or lectures in the way in which we do by seeing ourselves in this theatrical context in terms of our role and their role, and the ways in which we may manage this theatricality of the occasion. We are re-confirming that we can actually, as sociologists, speak sensibly and with meaning and significance about social reality. We are trying to strike a bargain, an agreement between the teacher and the taught and that they join in affirming that organised talking in sociology, just like we're doing now, just as happens in classrooms and lectures and seminars, can reflect express, delineate, portray, if not completely come to grips with the real world, and that finally there is a real structured somewhat unitary world out there to comprehend.

References
Goffman K. The Lecture: in Forms of Talk, 1981.

Summary of Astley Discussion

The discussion was largely concerned with the relative merits of the content of the lecture or seminar and the effectiveness of its presentation. Those who ar-gued for the elevation of presentation to equal status with content claimed that to teach anything means that presentation is as important as content. Communi-cation skills can and should be developed in order to efficiently transmit to the audience exactly what the speaker has in mind.

There was also a need for flexibility of style so as to take into account the ex-pectations of the audience. The teacher of sociology must spend time building up the audience's self-confidence so that a dialogue could take place. Sociology is a subject which should invite discussion: "we are not handing down tablets to the class". (Astley).

One speaker claimed that the discussion was blurring the distinction between teacher and lecturer. In HE in particular there was a noticeable disdain for teaching that many considered to be work of a lower status than research, but even if that were true, and many thought that it was not, what was the good of the research if it was not effectively communicated?

As this talk clearly shows I was then, and remain, keen to understand why and how educational practitioners do their talking. In my later speculations about the nature of professional practitioners in 'the people industries' I have empha-sised that due consideration should be given to how we talk, to colleagues, and to our clients whoever they may be. Indeed, in my 2018 book 'The role of so-cial science in the education of professional practitioners' a good deal of time is devoted to exploring the essential nature of talking in our daily social-interactions with colleagues and clients. My main aim in that study was for 'trainee' professionals, whether they were intending to be teachers of various kinds, or social workers, or health care workers and so on, should come to un-derstand how essential is was 'to make sense of themselves'. We should all do this on a daily basis, but, if you are someone who intends to give service to cli-ents it is essential to be knowledgeable, and empathetic to those clients' needs, but also to be an effective and efficient communicator. Talking should not only convey information and ideas within particular situations, but create a contact, 'build bridges' that allow understanding and engagement.

In the 1980s I was asked to give a talk at the annual conference of The Leisure Studies Association; they were doing a 'state of youth' event. I have included below the transcript of my talk; 'Take a walk on the wild side: leisure and pop music in a commercial world.' I opened my presentation by playing three pop songs, 'Wild Boys' by Duran Duran, 'Take a walk on the wild side' by Lou Reed, and 'Invisible Sun' by The Police. My aim here, apart from pop music entertainment of course, was to move from a shallow pop song most definitely not about wild boys, to The Police's very dark song about young people in Northern Ireland in 'The Troubles'.

It was clear that my talk came as a shock to the delegates, with the Q & A, and talk in the bar afterward, concentrating on 'did I really mean what I had said?'

Take a walk on the it side'

Leisure and pop music in a commercial world

Daniel Farson in his early 60's TV series 'Living for Kicks' identified an important new phenomenon, the teenage consumer. Farson echoed the conventional wisdom of the day by arguing that the new spending and free living power of the young meant the arrival/confirmation even of a new kind of teen-ager:..."enjoying himself - or fails to enjoy himself - in a completely new way." At the heart (in a heartless world?) of this new way of life this youth/teenager culture was the buying of pleasure and the pursuit of leisure. To be permitted to spend their lives in this way was clearly seen as the greatest gesture the young could make in gratitude for the post-war settlement - of the formation of the welfare state. Farson went further though, looking beyond the euphoria and bonhomie he identified - as a concerned well educated adult would - a few problems associated with this liberation. The mass of these

teen-age consumers are no problem says Farson (sic) however there is that
minority who on the one hand are not enjoying them-selves, not joining in,
while there are also those who go too far and spoil the fun, not only for their
peers but also for the non-combatants, the grown-ups. Fyvel (1), like many
other early ob-servers of post-war youth found in these 'insecure offenders' a
source of much adult breast-beating'

This is common knowledge amongst those persons attending a conference
such as this. We are all well used to the mass/youth culture debate, the
consumer so-ciety/labour politics dilemmas, the concern over the uses of
literacy, the great commercial swindle/money trick etc. I do not intend to
recapitulate on this lit-erature and debate, other than to comment on the
grave dangers of taking for granted the conventional wisdoms of our own
collective analyses of what post war British society has done to the children
of the welfare state.

One of our problems, as youth workers, administrators, sociologists,
teachers and the like, is our weakness and fragility in the face of the constant
pressure to stay on the leisure/pleasure merry-go-round.

A great deal has been written in the 1980's about the/a lost generation.
Much heart-searching has gone on - particularly in the labour movement and
its fel-low travelling pop analysis, media-orientated and paid-up members
of the Peter Pan Club Circles. What has happened to the present younger
generation? How have they been affected by the recession, by Thatcherism,
by being forced to live in Giro City ever nearer to that 'Clockwork Orange'
nightmare etc? Quite clearly we are not only worried about them, we are also
worried about our-selves. We should be; we should be concerned about our
role in the formation of the present state of social and cultural relations that
is part and parcel of what young persons call everyday life.

There are inevitably many ifs and buts here. If post-war British society
had not moved towards a welfare state on the one hand and an increasing
consumer led economic expansion on the other, would young people have had

what scope they did? If numerous forms of American popular culture had not penetrated UK air space so soon would there have been the increasingly precocious musi-cal developments here? If the collective war-fare to welfare spirit had not pre-vailed would there have been so much for the young to have and be resented for?

There can be little doubt that the economic and socio-political developments that took place after 1942 say created a degree of 'space' that allowed the for-mation of a post-war generation of 'youth' plus the associated enthusiasm, creation, mediation, adoption etc. of distinctive looking and sounding cultures. So it could be argued that the post war generation were 'found' in possession of much lethal equipment with which to perpetrate their grotesque and dastardly deeds up to and including the 1960's. The post-war generations direct effect on youth and music cultures came to an end in the middish 1960's. From that point the starting place for much of the inter-relation between youth and music shift-ed to another site. This is not to say that the traditions, some important values, cultural patterns etc of the post-war scene were completely thrown out; far from it. They were in a residual culture sense relocated within the aspects of emergent pop, youth and music cultures that developed.

Indeed, it goes further than this. Much of the recent discussion of youth has been with their identity and direction crisis. 'Nihilism is the message in words and music', 'Skinheads and the search for white working class identity' 'The mystery of the disappearing radical young', 'Dole queue rock' etc. etc. It almost seems as if the 'Folk devils' have sold out their birth right and have taken up a position uncomfortably suspended between shoulder shrugging pusillanmouness and 'mindless' cultural cannibalism. The social critique that we recognized in ourselves in that 'Folk devil' golden age seems lost now under the avalanche of regrettable circumstances that comprises the last decade or so: What haunts us now is the recognition that our pop/leisure pleasure - the kind perhaps we wish could still be vibrant today, might have been merely a commodity fix! That it was not 'just' that we ye.re the hopeless or even self-deluding victims of Ideo-logical State Apparatuses but _ also of Ideological Consumer Apparatuses! What I want to ask is whether we can come to terms with the ending or passing of a set of conditions that gave us in the 60's etc., the space to be wild. Can we, now, given our standing, help create ways in which young people can be more wild than they are, but perhaps direct their wildness into social critique and even action for the good society? We certainly do have to recognize that many people, including the young are so beyond the influences of our socialist - lib-eral critique/frame of reference, that they will take action that will upset, of-fend and injure us. We have often contributed to a situation where they have been deprived of even minimal rights - let alone any real notion of citizenship - we can hardly expect them to be nice about it

A year or so ago I heard an economist argue that the two faster growing sectors of employment in the UK were security firms and sports and leisure centres. Might we soon find ourselves as closely guarded sports enthusiasts, while, 'be-yond the pale' many (young) people take their pleasures, in anti-social ways?

Part of our crisis of pop/media/leisure is that we don't have enough of 'one man's meat and another man's poison', we are fed endless formula pop! Wild Boys' aren't really being wild - at least not in the comfort of our own homes. 'Taking a walk on the wild side' indicates to me the need for us to set into mo-tion some thorough-going deviance that sends the establishment and privileged layers in our society into a moral and cultural panic the like of which we have not seen let alone experienced for a long time.

****

Another example of my own practice might emphasise this point. For several years in the 1980/90s I was a tutor at social science summer schools which formed part of Open University degree courses. I was also teaching my usual undergraduate courses during term time, but considered the work of the OU to be very important, and was therefore very happy to be involved in these week long summer schools. OU students were, and still are, 'distance learners', based and studying at home. They do have regular contact and even group meetings with an OU tutor in their locality, but the one major opportunity to spend time on a conventional university campus was at summer school. In my experience most students relished this opportunity to mix with like-minded students, and 'soaked up' the atmosphere including the chance to be on a real university campus! In addition to the daily course related classes students also had the op-tion to attend evening talks given by tutors like me on subjects of particular in-terest to those tutors.

For several years I had the pleasure of giving a regularly updated talk on 'Six propositions about culture and identity'. These talks (and they were deliberately talks and not 'lectures') always provoked intense, interested, debates. The dia-logue rumbled on afterward, usually in the bar, for some time, and I always felt that they unleashed a genuine desire among a very diverse group of people to discuss and speculate about contemporary society and utopian visions. The very openness of such culturally heterogeneous groups of people brought to-gether in a wonderful educational spirit always seemed to me to be resources for hope. It was the 'invitation to talk'; openly, speculatively, seriously and without a feeling of it being unusual or odd (which OU students of commented on feeling about their daily lives) that was so rewarding. Talking can do that, perhaps much more so than just reading a book, or being told things?

There are two further examples I would mention here. Firstly, devising an adult education evening class for the Workers Educational Association (WEA) on the life and work of William Morris. In the six weeks of this course, with a student group of about ten students, we covered a great deal on Morris as poet, designer, writer, journalist and socialist. At the end of the course I asked the group if they were pleased with what we had covered one student said yes, he was very pleased, but thought that I had not told them everything that I knew about Morris!

I suggested that I had to leave some scope for them to pursue their own study.

The second example was with an Introduction to Philosophy course that went so well that the students asked for further course more focused on Ethics. This we did, with the increasing the role of students reading particular texts and pre-senting their thoughts to the group. There was some reluctance initially from some students to take on this task, but eventually nearly everyone did. A badge of honour perhaps? What these interactive sessions emphasised was the role of talking, highlighting the social-interaction, and as I pointed out our using the Socratic method, a dialectical approach to learning through discussion and de-bate.

After doing at least three different courses with this particular student group I told them that other commitments meant that I would have to stop. They were disappointed, but I argued that as they had become so proficient they no longer needed me and could run the classes themselves. Which they did!

I learnt a great deal from devising and teaching these classes over several years, including coming to understand much more about the learning processes of adults as distinct from children, andragogy rather than pedagogy.

Not the least of the issues here was the way that adult students will bring their life experiences to any class, and with encouragement and good planning will draw on that experience of everyday life to develop their understanding and put these ideas in context. This becomes a resource; learnt skills, self-confidence, to take forward in to future educational pursuits, and life. The students took own-ership of these processes, promoting their own agency.

Another dimension of these events, is that they were events, special occasions. Many students were eager to enter into a discussion about the alienating aspects of everyday life, along with the endless paradoxes of living a life, the absurdi-ties of it all. Of course studying Philosophy was a significant contribution to this learning process. Emphasising the paradoxes and those absurdities of eve-ryday life!

They may not have seen themselves as surrealists, but they understood the is-sues well enough. They also understood that strategies and tactics were needed on a daily basis, circumvent the daily realities of living in a 'snakes and lad-ders' society.

I say more about these issues in my section on Adult Education later in this es-say.

While on the subject of surrealists, it is worth mentioning in passing some of the contexts that do relate importantly to the discussion about arts and cultural development.

Responses to the 1914-18 war were understandably mixed amongst the 'artis-tic' and intellectual circles of Europe and North America, and I am sure in oth-er parts of the world as well. Certainly there was a great questioning about the possible, any possible, future for humanity, or even more narrowly, civilisa-tion, after the 'irrational' inhumanity of the War. Thinking on this question was largely split between those who sought to promote utopian solutions, and the prospects for socialism and even communism was a major response. As Marx had said the choice between Communism or Barbarism. It was evident that the possibility of an industrial modernity driven by Bourgeois values; lib-erty, equality and fraternity; was impossible. There were those who argued that given the demonstrated fallibility of human beings, realism based on reform based on reason was the only option. And, then there those who sought to em-phasise the absurdity of modern life given that everyday life was increasingly degraded and routinized affecting any person's capacity for autonomous action and creative self-expression. To bring people to 'their senses'; plenty of Freud in here; and even aid the stripping away of a false consciousness ala Marx, an alternative take on the human condition was essential.

There was also in this mix a turn away from the 'certainties' of established, and mainly figurative manifestations of the art of modernity. One response, notably in the USA was the emergence of abstract expressionism, Jackson Pollock and his associates. It is also possible to argue that the home promotion of abstract expressionism served as a sharp, and political, contrast to the imposition of the Socialist Realism of Stalinism. Both artistic 'solutions' being ideological.

So, as I have already suggested, especially in my conference talk above, I have tried to place equal value on writing and talking throughout my practice. It is inevitable that academic life will take a person into the world of conferences, giving 'papers' i.e. talks, and doing a lot of listening and ad hoc interventions. Plus, of course as already suggested a great deal, perhaps too much (?) in the informal settings of such events, as I suggested in my reference to OU Summer Schools. In fact on reflection I would suggest that some of the best conferences I have attended the most interesting and rewarding parts were in informal; in the bar, meal times etcetera. Referencing Goffman, and what in my experience many 'Theatricals' say, is that there is a lot of 'business' going on. 'Situations' yet again.

Certainly as for a the more specific world of 'the arts' I have spent a great deal of time doing formal and informal talks, interventions, responses and so on, at meetings with all manner of people and organisational settings in the world of arts and culture.

Writing on Culture

My more specific writing about Culture, and cultural artefacts began in the 1970s. I certainly wrote about many cultural issues before then as some aspect of my student life in sociology, philosophy, social and political history, and education studies. I certainly did in my late 60s/early70s research on the 'Secu-larist Movement in London in the 1860s.', but the focus was incidental to the main academic course in hand. It was only when I actually entered the educa-tion profession in 1973 that I chose to write much more specifically about Cul-ture. I had by then read and absorbed in to my world view John Ruskin, Wil-liam Morris and their contemporaries in the second half of the nineteenth cen-tury, and then later writers already discussed in this essay; Williams, Thompson and Hoggart, and all their contemporaries. While I was writing my dissertation on 'The Secularists' I discovered Richard Altick's wonderful study, 'The Eng-lish Common Reader', first published in 1957; it was the first comprehensive study of how the majority of people came to read, and how this helped to 'make' them as cultural agents, so being more in control of the knowledge and understanding of cultural issues in order to be creative, and make their own way in life; a vibrant history of self-help and autodidacts. This optimistic read-ing of the situation does have to be set against the prevailing tendency for peo-ple to be defined by their possibilities, and daily confined by the structures of consent which hang over lives like a persistent fog.

As part of my practice as a Sociologist and Educationalist I wrote small and big stuff on culture in general and the endless variety of pieces on specific is-sues, people and artefacts. I wrote a good deal about the cultures of young peo-ple; class, gender, ethnicity, neighbourhood/place/locality, musical subcultures, argot, and so on. A good deal of this enquiry went in to my late 1970s book 'Why Don't We Do It in The Road' on the Beatles Phenomenon. This was a contextual study, asking questions about how a cultural phenomenon like The Beatles could happen. Chapter 4 was 'Youth' where I attempted a comprehen-sive account of who young people are, how did they get to be like that, what was the nature of the myriad of youth cultures and so on. I discussed a consid-erable range of both academic and non-academic studies, and of course drew on my own experience of being a teenager in the 1960s. (I am more or less the same age as The Beatles) I spent some time in that book working through many issues on how to approach the study of culture(s), what methods of re-search/study could be used, and how this would in turn contextualise studies like the one on The Beatles. As I said at the time of writing;

'If we take a detached, long-term view of The Beatles phenomenon, then the tendency is to stand outside of the phenomenon in an attempt to produce analy-sis. But there are, of course, great dangers here, particularly perhaps in losing sight of the dialectical process by which these historical phenomenon, event, came about. If, however, we adopt a close-up, biographical approach, we en-counter difficulties with placing too much emphasis upon them, The Beatles, losing sight of the overall passage of time and the overall significance of events – past, present and future.' (Astley 2006 p.188)

Theoretically this was foundational work for me, and my core focus on the in-ter-relation between the social structures of everyday life, like family, class, neighbourhood and schooling, and our specific cultures, and our own biog-raphy, contributed to who we are, and might be. And, all this is happening over time, and my approach to the specificity of The Beatles Phenomenon, as with all my work, indicates an historicist approach, an emphasis on the im-portance of history in understanding values and the determination of events, cultural phenomenon.

Of course any person's research orientation, why they are interested in doing what they do, is reflected in their work. It is self-consciously or otherwise, part of their conditions of practice, and writing on Culture in last fifty years has certainly exemplified that;

'...what we see now much more regularly is a desire by researchers and writers to focus attention upon cultural products. There is a steady stream of writing on the culture industries, and in a Williams-ish way a concern about the conditions of production in those industries. There is a tendency in some of this writing to de-politicise the issues; indeed, a valid criticism of some cultural studies is the emergence of an apolitical posture, which seeks to separate scholarship from the everyday consequences of social relationships dominated by inequalities of power.' (Astley 2006 p.9)

By the mid-1980s my interest in theoretically, and direct academic/teaching in-volvement with the degree level education of professional practitioners in so-cial and welfare roles, came together much more. My work with designing and delivering curricula for nurses and midwives, social workers, youth workers and others took up more of my thinking and doing time. A good example of my own praxis at this time was taking my theoretical work, with youth policy course development into my local community to work with youth and commu-nity provision. With a community worker colleague, we established The Ado-lescent Network which brought together a very diverse range of people in my locality whose professional practice was with children and young people. We also created a regular bulletin of information and news on policy and practice which I edited. This venture was very successful, going a long way to integrat-ing thinking and doing, and establishing a communications infrastructure that supported all involved, and we were sure led to better service provision for our clients.

In many ways John O'Neill summed up this very well;

'In my view sociology is a symbiotic science. Its promise is to give back to people what it takes from them. This is true of all culture but sociology more than any other discipline promises to make this a practical truth.' (O'Neill 1972 p.7)

O'Neill's values are reflected in my own practice, and emphasises that for

127

many of us our action research methodology; a dialectic of feeding evi-dence/ knowledge from field work research directly back to the people in ques-tion to enrich their lives. They are the subjects, not merely objects, of the re-search.

In all my work with aspiring professional practitioners I sought to aid them to 'make sense of themselves' before they could take on the complex and often paradoxical task of making sense of their client's needs, and the contexts that create those needs and directly affect the nature and outcomes of interventions. (see Astley 2020)

My own work on youth cultures, policy and practice was taken into my creat-ing a degree pathway on Youth Policy. Some of the essays which I had already written on youth cultures, music and so on, went in to course reader which I wrote for my students.

In all of these ways there was self-consciously, a constant link between theory and practice. My theoretical development, especially in the field of culture, my engagement with those theories already in the public domain, and my other, dual practice, as a teacher came together.

Writing on culture for my local community

One of the important aspects of my writing about culture is a series of articles I have written for my local weekly newspaper The Exmouth Journal. Some years ago I started a weekly column the 'Community Education Column' because I had things to say about the contemporary issues that contextualised people's everyday lives. I also wanted to offer local people of a very diverse kind to have the opportunity to write about their own practice and take on local events. I am pleased to say that many people took that opportunity and appeared in print for the first time. Of course I helped by giving guidelines and doing some judicious editing.

More recently I have been writing a series of pieces on aspects of Culture for column, and some of these appear below. The main impetus for writing these articles was the creation of Arts & Culture East Devon (ACED) a forum of 'artists' in a very wide sense who have come together to talk about the role of the arts in our area. We have also spent some time discussing the infrastructure needs of practising artists. We now have a Council led Arts & Culture Strategy, setting out a ten-year programme for developing the arts in East Devon, putting a lot of this talking in to practical action,

Arts & Culture in East Devon; the developing picture.

Readers of this column will be familiar with my pieces on art and culture, for example 'Problems with Art' (June), 'Champions of art and culture help connect communities' (October) and 'Art and Nature' (November).

All of these pieces were linked to my role of Education Champion for Arts and Culture East Devon (ACED) which has made a good start in bringing together artists in the widest sense, to discuss their own practice, and, crucially their role and how it is played in the everyday life of East Devon.

129

You may know that EDDC has now taken this Arts & Culture initiative a step further by inviting responses to a call for tenders for the new East Devon Culture Strategy. (Go to the EDDC, or Thelma Hulbert Gallery (Honiton) websites for details.

The tender documents reiterate the aims, aspirations and priorities of the East Devon Culture Strategy;

1.   Better homes and communities for all
2.   Greener East Devon
3.   A resilient economy

The documents, with quotes from Councillor Nick Hookway, EDDC portfolio holder for tourism, sport, leisure and culture, emphasise the social and economic value of the arts and heritage industries to East Devon.

This whole initiative raises many key questions about the nature of arts and culture; or perhaps that should be culture and the arts; in East Devon. There are some institutional arts and culture agents already established in that locality, but there are also a very large and diverse number of artists of many practices across our communities. Many of these individuals, and small scale organisations, are actively engaged in creating and promoting the arts within our communities. The diversity of artists who are currently members of the ACED network is impressive, and they bring a great deal to this new cultural strategy. They are also looking forward to the successful implementation of the Arts & Culture strategy to help them to continue, and develop as practicing artists.

At our most recent Network Forum meeting a good deal was said about the Creative Industries, which is a term that covers a range of economic activities which are concerned with the generation and exploitation of knowledge, information, and artistic endeavour across a wide spectrum. This approach reflects the idea that human creativity is the ultimate economic resource, on a personal and social scale. This seems to be at the heart of the EDDC strategy.

However, we also need to consider the idea of the Culture Industries; a more focussed generalisation of the way artists works within a range of everyday conditions that affect their practice. Are with talking about the solo painter or illustrator, the musician, the film maker, the dancer or singer, local galleries, the cinema, the local theatre groups and so on? They are all economically active, it is their labour and livelihood; but it is also their vocation, the way in which their aesthetic values drive them to do what they do.

So, the motives of those engaged with art and culture are inevitably diverse, with some practitioners and organisations being much more profit driven than others. Many artists in East Devon have created a CIC or Social Enterprise, through which to do their work in a not-for-profit manner. Many artists are very wary of the manner in which the profit motive often trumps aesthetic values.

The idea of Culture is also central to this arts and culture strategy, because I would argue that 'culture is ordinary'; it is the lived culture of a particular time and place, our everyday lives which includes our creative and artistic labour. 'Our' culture also has a history to it, and usually with most artists, ideas about what a future social life should be like, could be like, given more leadership and encouragement. More opportunities, support and access to resources, and less bureaucracy!

So, all of these issues, ideas and arguments about aims, motives and the like, will need to be discussed, and decisions made in the most democratic way possible. Don't be left out of this discussion!
John Astley   12/21

East Devon Cultural Strategy.

In January (5.1.22) I wrote in these pages about the EDDC's arts and culture strategy, and in particular about the Council seeking consultants for their/our 'ten-year cultural strategy'. Festival & Events International (FEI) were chosen as the consultants, and their work for EDDC was launched at a meeting of the Arts & Culture East Devon (ACED) group on 7th February at the wonderful Beehive arts centre in Honiton.

I am writing now with an update, a work in progress report. However, before doing that update it is important to remind ourselves why this work needs doing. I could do worse than quote Peter Abbs (1996);

'In our society we have failed to develop any adequate public conception of the true significance of the arts. They exist not necessarily on the margins but always in an indeterminate state, constantly distorted by extraneous demands, curious expectations and fundamental misunderstandings. Under the controlling forces of a market economy the arts are invariably placed under the banner of leisure and consumption; they become commodities, competing with other commodities in the hustle and bustle of the market place. In education, similarly, they are misplaced and misunderstood, not generally envisaged as possessing the same value as the Humanities and Sciences.'

Considering these issues, focusing on change, and putting things right, is a key aspect of this Cultural Strategy, the work of ACED, and certainly part of my role as Education Champion.

And, while I am here, I should also mention a new publication of my own; 'Tragedy in our Everyday Lives: The Role of Popular Culture'. This 90-page monograph focusses particularly on TV drama, and discusses the value of TV drama in its many formats, considering future prospects and possibilities. I have written this essay with the general reader in mind, but also to be used as a resource for teachers and students of theatre and drama studies.

If anyone would like to access a copy they can contact me at astley.john@

gmail.com or 07713606273.

Art and Nature.
John Astley 10/21

With impeccable timing (Cop26 and G20 meetings) BBC4 has just finished broadcasting the three-part series 'Nature and Us: A History through Art', and of course the series is now accessible via BBC iPlayer.

The series was written and presented by James Fox, an historian of art, who has often appeared on TV with stimulating programmes. He also put in a brief appearance on-line for the recent Budleigh Literary Festival (www. budlitfest.org.uk). He was interviewed about his new book on 'Colour', and very good it is too.

For anyone who is interested in the history of art since cave painting to now, and concerned with climate change, and, fascinated by the way we humans have regarded, valued and related to Nature, or not, should watch these programmes.

As we expect now the visual aspects of the programme are stunning, but it is also the way Fox draws our attention to the dynamics of our often paradoxical relationship with Nature that makes this series so enthralling and educational. All three programmes have a lot to offer the viewer, but the third and final part, looking at the Twentieth Century, makes for a salutary experience. What have we done? What are 'we' still doing, or not?

A good deal of what Fox has to say focuses on the significance of our day to day cultural understanding of, and creative responses to Nature. Understandably his perspective is global, and he inevitably discusses the dominant ideas that have motivated human beings over time. For example, he, and his expert guests, reflect upon the obsession with progress. What constitutes progress he asks; ever rapidly changing technological innovation, a determination to have control over Nature in all respects, and a reckless disregard for the intended and unintended consequences of our actions.

In this last programme he brings discussion of the Anthropocene in to perspective, the epoch of Humankind. This proposed geological epoch has become a regular theme in discussions about the impact that human beings have had on Nature, understandably drawing comparisons with changes to Nature before and after we arrived on the scene. But, with a particular emphasis on the period since the mid Twentieth Century, and the Atomic age, and the astonishing acceleration of urbanisation across the planet. The pressures we continue to exert on Earth has gone so far that the very continued existence of the planet, let alone the population of the world, is at risk. Wikipedia has a very useful twenty-page introduction to this concept, which considers the lack of focus on the role of global capitalism, imperialism and racism.

Of course selfishness and greed has made a major contribution to the mess we are now in, and, belatedly addressing despite all the warnings that have been given over many decades. Human's (okay not all of us!) obsession with economic growth and control over, and manipulation of Nature/natural resources, has created havoc, and embedded in our cultures a set of values that are now increasingly challenged. The desire for control over Nature ranges from the very English fetish with 'the lawn', to an on-going ravaging of the countryside to meet our everyday consumer and comfort wants.

There are of course some glimmers of hope, with values and attitudes changing. For example, people deciding to re-use and repair, rather than buy new in an endless cycle of built-in obsolescence and waste.

Fox looks at contemporary artists using their creativity to make a point. There have been many more insights in to the extent of this crisis, often from TV programmes, on issues around biodiversity, climate, and weather.

Locally, Transition Exmouth has raised awareness, while emphasising what we can all do on a daily basis. Even in the last few weeks, articles have appeared in the Exmouth Journal dealing with specific issues all linked to Climate Change. Clearly we need such consciousness raising to increase because even when we stop to look and listen to the arguments, and try to understand what is at stake, the enormity of it all can be very daunting; what can I do? So, returning to James Fox's series, what can local artists in the broadest sense do to help our awareness and understanding?

Problems with Art.

Besides being a pictorial joy for many people, Art can often be a problem, difficult to understand. What is it for? Is it, should it be, a clear and self-consciously a representation of the (real) world in which we observers live? If this is so, why do we need it? We have a chair; why do we need a picture of one? We live in a landscape, by the sea, or next to a factory, why have another one hanging on the wall, or even more ostentatiously in a gallery or other public space?

What of the artist? What is their intention in creating this 'work'; i.e. expending their labour? Is this to engage us in reminiscence, a pleasurable sensation of colour, subject matter, touch, joy, anger and so on? Is the artist conveying some message to us, about ourselves, the world in which we live, the state of humanity, about themselves, their inner-most hopes and fears?

Does it make any difference to us what form the art work in in? Is a painting, or a sculpture, or photograph, or a film, a play, or a song, all much the same when it comes to assessing the value of the cultural artefact, to the artist, to us, to society in general, the market place for art works?

Does it matter what form the art work takes? Is this often fashion, a sign of the times? And, does the value of these arts works depend on how much people are prepared to pay for them, for these 'objects' to become their

135

private property?

Faced with the wide variety of art works, past and present, people often say 'I know what I like', but why do they like it, and equally dislike something else? And how and why do they know this? Is this due to their personal taste in matters of art aligned to their taste in everyday life things in general; food, clothes, people, sports and so on. It may be that people's preferences in art are mainly a factor of their family life, their education, or their gender, social class or cultural group? Those key aspects of our everyday lives that shape our values.

Can art change us, as individuals, socially? Can, do we, change it, meaning and value by the very act of engaging with it; rendering the appreciation of art an inter-active process. So, should art reflect change, record it for posterity, or, challenge the status quo, highlight injustices, demand change? Be in the vanguard of personal and collective transformation, creating thinking and doing spaces to discuss, debate, argue over? Or, is this over theorising the meaning and value of art, as since the late nineteenth century at least, Oscar Wilde and others in the Aesthetic Movement, proclaimed 'art for art's sake'!

So, lots of questions, what about some answers, the answers?

Many very clever and creative people have argued over these questions, about what art is and what it is for; even what it could be for. Is this a vital part of our education, talking and, perhaps, more importantly, doing it!

For me the educational dimension is essential to our making, and using art; skills to learn and practice, appreciation of the contexts of the creation of art, and engagement. Enlightenment, part of a civilising process?

John Astley 6/21

East Devon's 'Cultural Strategy' is under way!

In January this year I used this Community Education Column to outline the EDDC's plans to create, and develop an Arts & Culture Strategy. As many readers will know the Cultural Strategy 2022 – 2031 has now been published, and the aim of this article is to bring you up to date with developments, and, encourage your involvement.

The Strategy document emphasised the core values that underpinned the initiative that the Strategy should be Collaborative, Diverse and inclusive, Resilient, and Connected with nature. There are also eight Themes that encapsulate the aims of the Strategy; Strengthen and support 'people-that-do', Protect and enhance the natural environment, Cultural tourism, Creative enterprise and skills, New places for culture (e.g. an Arts Centre for Exmouth?), Connectivity, Cultural leadership, and to 'Capture the value' that could ensure learning and improvement by monitoring and evaluating the change that creativity and culture has on people and place. As the Education champion of Arts & Culture East Devon (ACED) I am certainly focused on all of these themes.

Under the leadership of councillor Nick Hookway, EDDC appointed consultants to seek out the views, ideas and concerns of a wide range of people in East Devon, and to make recommendations on the Strategy and its development. That Report is now in the public domain, and one of the key outcomes is the appointment of a Cultural Producer to help lead the Strategy over the next decade. Sarah Elghady will take up her role in January, and all of us in the ACED Forum are looking forward to working with her in developing the Strategy in conjunction with the citizens in East Devon.

The ACED Forum has already begun the process of bringing people together, making important connections, sharing experience, and developing ideas. Ruth, Fiona, and the team based at the Thelma Hulbert Gallery in Honiton have done that in organising meetings and events, creating a soon

137

to be launched website, and setting up a Facebook page. All of this activity over recent months, during and since the 'pandemic' has emphasised a core aspect of the Strategy, to develop an arts producers' infrastructure. To support, encourage, inform, and promote all the arts and art practitioners in East Devon.

EDDC have emphasised that East Devon is a very popular destination for visitors throughout the year. The consultants research showed that many visitors seek out and enjoy the arts in the widest sense; why wouldn't they! There is so much to see and do; museums, galleries, festivals, a vibrant music scene, engagement with those producing art products, along with many other ways to engage with the creative cultures of East Devon. The recent opening of Anna Fitzgerald's Sea Dog Art Café on the Fountain roundabout in Exmouth, is yet another example of recent developments. The creative 'industries' are set to get even busier.

And, our culture does matter; it is central to an understanding of who we are, our identity and values. The Arts do have a way of enlightening and shedding light in these dark days. The recent wonderful BBC2 series 'Art That Made Us' demonstrated how, when and why artists use their creativity to describe, explain and challenge the society of our everyday lives. (This series is now on BBC iPlayer)

So, much has already been done, but there is a lot more to do. This Strategy for Arts & Culture is an opportunity for all of us in East Devon to engage, and to take some responsibility for developing our creativity, individually and collectively.

With the help of the editorial staff at the Exmouth Journal I am hoping to use this Community Education Column to share your ideas. Let me know: astley.john@gmail.com or 07713606273

Thinking about Culture.
John Astley 12/22

As a sociologist it is inevitable that using theory plays an important role in my daily practice. And, there are plenty of theories in use with explanations of Culture!

So, continuing on from my recent piece on the East Devon Cultural Strategy (Exmouth Journal 21/12) I thought it might be useful to mention some basic ideas as we come to terms with our individual and collective role in developing the Cultural Strategy in this New Year. Of course I am always happy to elaborate!

Culture is a process, being creatively made and re-made, as well as a collection of artifacts; a painting, a piece of music, a novel, a pair of jeans, a tattoo. In turn these, and many other artifacts are endowed with historically, and the value of such artifacts determined by powerful ideas. (even ideas about 'high art/the canon, and 'low art/popular).

Culture should therefore be understood as a 'verb' as well as a 'noun'. Culture is not just a thing, a commodity, it is also about creativity, about making, involving human labour as well as ideas.

So, Culture can be regarded as a field on interaction between;

1. People's social relationships, conventions and customs. This includes a consideration for the centrality of social institutions, e.g. family.
2. The symbolic forms (e.g. language, or visual, or musical representations) available to them for focusing on, and co-ordinating experience.
3. People's systems of beliefs, values and actions.
4. Their judgements about the good, bad, beautiful and ugly. These personal and collective 'grass roots' judgements can be seen as a 'grounded aesthetic', i.e. not just those handed down in some canon.

Indeed, there are invariably arguments around giving of value for any cultural artifact. These are 'sites of struggle' in everyday life and culture. The expression of these fought over and/or negotiated departures from the canon is usually understood as style.

Part of the process of Culture is the ongoing debate around relevant and meaningful discourses; who says what to whom and under what conditions. A vocabulary of motives. The grounded aesthetics aspect is also important here in that the means via which people can express, and do their cultural creativity is invariably in a DIY manner; using, adapting and modifying existing technologies, symbol forms (like language) and so on. Culture is ordinary, and special. There is also a concern with both the process of Culture, human creativity and so on, and with the organisation and conditions of production of any cultural artifact. What are the conditions that dictate the practice of any 'artist'? We all make culture, but not necessarily in conditions of our own choosing.

Towards the end of my recent article I mentioned the 'Creative Industries', and these big scale producers of our culture continue to play a major part in our everyday lives. They are so pervasive, so normal, we do tend to take them for granted. The products of the media, especially perhaps TV, in all its contemporary forms, is an appropriate example. But, also the Press, which you are reading now. And, what about the music industries, 'social media' sites, and so on? If we take a few minutes to consider these cultural artifacts, and how we use them, we can for example ask who owns these 'industries'? What appear to be the motives behind this production, and the role of the variety of creative people that actually do the work? How much influence do we think these culture producers have on us, and other people? Do we have a say in how these cultural producers create and deliver their bits of culture, whose needs are being met?

These few, and many others questions about our individual and collective use of 'culture' do remind us of the complexity of everyday life!

140

Keep in touch. astley.john@gmail.com

Culture, the Arts and Change.

When I wrote my book on The Beatles Phenomenon in 1979, John Lennon had one more year to live. How was I to know? I did remark in my text that I was somewhat surprised that John, like many of his contemporaries had survived that long given their years of experimenting with a range of substances. Many of course did not survive which had partly informed my view.

My essay was only partly about the four performers themselves, plenty of glossy tributes, and hagiographies/biographies already existed. I wanted to seek an explanation for myself, and anyone else who was interested, about why, where and how a cultural phenomenon like The Beatles could happen. Indeed, in my thankfully relatively short book of 227 pages I did not get to my chapter The Beatles until page 119, chapter five of eight. The first four chapters focused on those cultural and social contexts, including chapters on Society and Culture, Liverpool in post-war Britain, and on Youth. Whether I did manage to satisfactorily explain that cultural phenomenon is left to the reader. But, one of the key concerns in that essay was about the tensions associated with social and cultural change, an historical process but with the specificity of time and place. A large part of my 'Beatles' study was about the responses made to those changes, especially the explicitly cultural ones. In terms of Liverpool in the 1950s and 60s the way musical ideas and inspirations were drawn from (carried across the Atlantic by the 'Cunard Yanks') the reflective and assertive range of music of the American diaspora; African Americans and the astonishing diversity of immigrants including so many Jews; all with their 'own' musical responses to change, and continuity. Of course many of the themes (life and loves, heartbreak, happiness, crushed male egos, alienation and so on) addressed by such groups of people were replicated in the white population, but not developed in same way. These cultural responses unleashed a cultural plurality that not only seriously upset the guardians of the cultural status quo, but opened a door to an opportunity to create, to make, and transform in line with an identity to suit the time redolent with ideas about the self and freedom. For most of these 'artists' creative output of their practice were transitional objects, the objective work, the painting, the tune, the photo and so on, that embodied their creativity, hopes and aspirations, and carried them through the 'sakes and ladders' of everyday life.

I should add a brief anecdote here; in the early 1980s a friend returned from a trip to Tokyo, and told me that on a visit to a bookshop found my 'Beatles' book on the Entomology shelves. Lost in translation again!

The reason I mention this now is in relation to the East Devon Arts & Culture Strategy that I have been discussing in these pages in recent weeks.

I have already emphasised that a key aim of this EDDC driven Strategy is as a democratic forum of, and for the Arts, as far as is possible and/or do-able. One very important aspect of this desire is to acknowledge that the arts in our area do not exist in a social, economic and political vacuum. Nor should they. Arts practitioners may be inspired, even driven, to do their work for many possible reasons, but they have to eat. Food comes before philosophy, or even music!

The Arts, individually and collectively, are cultural change, and affect cultural change, self-consciously or not. For example, we cannot assume that the market place for arts products, in the widest sense, in East Devon is on a 'level playing field'. Do all the arts practitioners in our community, from sole traders to organisations of various sizes, have the same 'footfall'? How informed, and/or discriminating are consumers, visitors of otherwise? Do they, can they, attract equal amounts of funding and sponsorship? I would suggest that this is one of the issues at the heart of the Arts & Culture Strategy.

At the national level of the Arts we have seen the recent decisions of The

Arts Council, a major funder, to reduce or remove funding, or change funding criteria, from some very 'high-end' arts organisations. The has happened recently to some providers of Opera. These changes have been linked to the governments 'levelling up' agenda, and has met with a mixed reception.

So, we can see ourselves, even 'find' ourselves, our true identity, in these cultural changes (remember being a teenager?). But we can also see our changing culture through ourselves, as a consequence of our actions and choices; come to understand how much our everyday lives have changed. The impact of the role of new technologies, design, image based advertising. and consuming come to mind.

In developing 'our' new Arts & Culture Strategy we should consider these inside out, and outside in aspects of change. This might help us all to make the best of the journey we are taking in East Devon.

Keep in touch;   astley.john@gmail.com 1/23

Adult Education

My community education column discussed and illustrated above, has been one aspect of my long standing commitment to Adult Education. In my late teens and early twenties, I benefitted from and contributed to what was then, in the 1960s a very lively Adult Education scene in the UK. My current commitment is essentially educational, in that what I write, encourage other people to write, and gain access, exposure, for this writing. In creating and hosting my Community Education Column for my local weekly newspaper I agree with the American John Dewey that learning is more important than a fixed and often turgid and domineering knowledge. I would also share Dewey's claim that education in the widest sense is the road to democracy. A really useful knowledge.

I was very politically engaged at that time, and also committed to trade union education. I learnt a great deal then about understanding the context in to which my own education and political activity should be seen. From the outset of my sociological education my focus was with community education, and educating the community, with a focus on social change. Many other people shared this experience, through the Workers Education Association (WEA), mentioned earlier, Adult Education provided by the Extra Mural Departments of universities, and, crucially, the Education Department of the Trades Union Congress (TUC). My experience at that time was it was the people working in this sector that really made the difference. Their educational role was not just a commitment to their subject specialisms, it was a desire to see people have access to, education, valuable bodies of knowledge, and the informed development of their own agency, belief in themselves and other like-minded people, to change life for the better. This was, and still is, a question of values, but for many participants, engagement with these cultures of education were an antidote for alienation, even praxis.

Or to paraphrase Alan Bennett; 'Pass it on boys, pass it on.' The raising of social consciousness was seen as a central value to be turned into action.

One again let me quote from Raymond Williams;

'There are two ways, perhaps, in which we can interpret the matter of the relation between Adult Education and social change. One, the evident and obvious one, is that Adult Education was instituted, developed and altered by social change in the sense of movements of the larger society. The other, less obvious but I think quite inner to its history, is that Adult Education offered to be, and at times was, part of the process of social change itself...Adult Education is the bottle with the message in it, bobbing on the tides and waves of history.' (Williams 1989 p.157)

This was for Williams, like many of us, the 'long revolution' of reform, social justice and democracy, which required people to be educated. It was also community based, and focused, certainly one aspect of Williams' 'structure of feeling', the ability of people within a community to understand the need for change through education opportunity, and the wherewithal to get on and do it!

Throughout my career as a teacher, whether I have devised the curriculum or not, I have been very aware of people's desire to be educated, both noun and verb forms, and with some encouragement from people like me, taking responsibility for their action. In almost all instances taking that first step across the threshold in to an educational milieu is really difficult. Empathy and practical support from tutors is vital, particularly in the dark moments of doubt.

This was for the proselytisers of (adult) education essentially a response to needs that were not being met by the State apparatus.

After 1944/5 the State engaged in some reforms to educational provision, with probably the most important for my generation increasing access to a Grammar School education. I was one of those children permitted to take a diagnostic intelligence test (the so called 11+) and make my way in to a leafy world of elbow patches and Gilbert & Sullivan. For me like so many others, an explanation of further and higher education also began, often a realisation that educational development involved a lot of self-help; welcome to the autodidacts world.

These reforms to educational reforms were of course one key part of the post-1945 Labour Government's creation of 'the welfare state', with its commitment to full employment, access to many more services and resources previously preserved for those with sufficient money to enter the market place and but whatever they needed or wanted. This widely shared, and welcomed social democratic approach to greater equality, and a degree of democracy, did lead many people to believe that the 'self-help' ethos of traditional adult education was not as necessary to ensure access to educational resources. However, by the 1960s when I entered the scene, attitudes had begun to change, a recognition that the State's educational largesse was actually very limited, and limiting.

And, putting my knowledge and use of theory in to practice.

Following on from my comments above about adult education in particular, but the entirety of this essay really, I need to consider my role in Arts and Culture East Devon (ACED). In the early years of the Coronavirus lock down in 2020 a group of arts oriented colleagues in East Devon, where I live, decided to set up ACED as a networking group for local arts and culture practitioners. We met regularly on zoom.

I was invited to become the Education Champion for the group, and have amongst other things written the series of newspaper articles re-printed above, raising issues about the value and role of art in our lives, and detailing information about ACED. The East Devon District Council decided that as a matter of policy they wished to go a step further and create a Cultural Strategy for East Devon. Their motivation has been primarily to support

146

local artists and art and culture providers to attract tourists to the area and boost economic growth. There are of course the usual commodification of art issues here, which will required continuous monitoring. The Council appointed consultants, and a wide ranging process of consulting local people and organisations took place. I was one of those interviewed. The report, 'Cultural Strategy 2022 – 2031' was published, much discussed, I wrote several newspaper articles about The Strategy, all included above. One of the key recommendations was to appoint a full time member of Council staff to the role of Cultural Producer, and this person came in to post at the beginning of 2023.

For me this a major step towards putting policy in to, and taking action on, the study of culture.

The nature of policy interventions has already been discussed in this essay, and the reality is still that the State, national and local continues to make interventions in to the making and, consuming of 'culture'. Exit through the gift shop is now the tourist norm. As other forms of money making, and employment decline, for example manufacturing, and farming, the rise of the service industry has risen. Tourism, and the so-called 'hospitality industry' is crucial to economic survival in these conventional ways. In my area many farmers have diversified in to B & B, and used their land for other purposes to make their assets viable, to 'work' for them, and location added value. The links here to 'Heritage' are obvious. 'Creatives' in general have become the next big money-making opportunity, and government has moved in to sponsorship etcetera, but only on their terms of course. There is also the aesthetics, and crucially life-style aspect of the artist as artisan, lending a measure of authenticity to commodities. This added value dimension to 'art goods' for the middle classes, comes for both producers and consumers, with the inevitable tensions between aesthetic and practice values and making an income, and growing the economy. No pressure then!

Since the creation of The Arts Council after the election of the Labour government in 1945 there has been a constant stream of funding, most of which has gone to London, or other metropolitan arts and culture organisations. This has essentially a measure to fund 'high culture' entertainments for the middle classes. Occasionally money has gone to quasi 'educational' ventures in order to keep the majority of people aware of what they should aspire to in the arts, making appropriate comparisons with their own lower status art. And, then there is the National Lottery, 'Good Causes', fleecing those whose making money and lifestyle aspirations drive them to gambling, which then ironically pay for middle class entertainments. Indeed, the 'working classes' have been left to access their arts entertainment etcetera via the commercial sector in a supply and demand market place relationship. A further example of the reality that we all have choices but not necessarily in conditions of our own choosing. As I have argued in my chapter on The Media, these provisions have created valuable in cash terms the Creative Industries to continue to play a major role in most people's lives.

My engagement with ACED was an opportunity to bring my knowledge of the study of culture; the use of theory, mine and other people's, to my broader interest in, and concern with the arts, and action taking. For me this was praxis, already discussed. Praxis refers in general to action, to focused and informed activity, and in this sense to be free, universal, creative action through which we make, produce and change, both shaping our historical world, and essentially, ourselves. As I have said before, 'making sense of ourselves', taking action in society in order to raise the consciousness of people in the process of change, the long revolution. Thinking, creativity, making and doing over time. The desire for truth, of ourselves and the world, is not a matter of mere contemplation, action is essentially based on what we know. Some of this action is the on-going enquiry in to everyday life, and coming to understand what it is we need to do next, imagining the future. As Richard Hoggart argued;

'We have to start with ourselves, with our own difficulties in saying what we mean, with finding a language fluent enough to express our individuality, or vulnerability, and our wish for direct and honest contact.' (Hoggart 1972 p.101)

This key issue accentuates what is called being reflexive, the recognition that researchers, writers and talkers are, and should be aware that they are making interventions in to people's lives by the action they take. This includes the researcher themselves, and therefore requires constant monitoring.

As I have argued throughout this essay, Cultural Studies as an approach to understanding is essentially about asking questions, setting-up and engaging in a discourse. Some of these questions will be driven by existing research and experience based knowledge, while some questions will be theory driven. This is a dialectical process, contrasting and comparing ideas and information before coming to a synthesis of knowledge. I, like many of my peers, have a body of skills and understandings, sometimes called techniques; the question is what do we do with all this? For many decades, researches in to our cultural lives have placed an emphasis on texts, as creative devices to understanding how we express ourselves. However, a good deal of such research has gone 'beyond' literary texts in one form or another, e.g. the novel, to explore others art forms. My own work on music is an example, where I have regularly pondered on how best to write in prose about an abstract art like music. Of course as a sociologist I can, and do as in my book on The Beatles, write about contexts; the social, economic, cultural, psychological and environmental aspects of people do creative things with music, producing and consuming. But can we really convey music in words, or pictures or...?

One of the key figures of Modernist thought about communication and culture was Georg Simmel, who lived in the second half of the nineteenth century and early twentieth. He was concerned with the social and cultural analysis of everyday life and was interested in the way people organised themselves, socially and economically in the emergent cities of Europe, and how this symbolic world mattered. One focus for him was that cultural organisation was in a two-way relation with social awareness of change, and identity. Thinking of Simmel's research, I am reminded how in the 1980s many city centres in the UK were transformed by the emerging gay culture, where music venues and cafes/bars with a concerted identity assertion vibe changed the townscape.

As I have discussed in this essay, there are many examples of where Modernism has promoted a set of ideas, not the least through the arts, about progress towards a better society and everyday life for all. The dominance of this liberal enlightenment has been there for all to see in the way we live, and the values we hold, but, this 'prophecy and progress' has only been intermittently delivered, often given and then when not convenient taken away again. This is where the arts have, and can raise a voice, challenge this reality to seek and find an alternative 'road-map'. Freedom for all is freedom for each.

In Sociology a key methodology is 'action theory' (very much an inheritance from Simmel and his contemporaries) the idea that in the course of research in to everyday life in the widest sense, the human beings we engage with are the subjects of study, and not objects. What is done by way of enquiry is primarily for them, and with them, the betterment of their/our lives and the society which is essentially communication. These are the roots of empathy. As Eagleton says;

'...the social-worker theory of morality has much to be said for it. There is much, morally speaking that we cannot judge about human beings, as we do not have the material conditions in which they might appear at their most virtuous. We have been observing them in extreme circumstances...' (Eagleton 1996 p.54)

In other words, the hegemonic values of high-end, elite, modernism that I discussed above has let them down by not meeting their basic needs for a reasonable standard of living, and fair and decent quality of life, and then blames them for it!

What all of these issues emphasises is a recurrent theme in this essay, namely that in Sociological analysis terms there is always going to be tension between the 'structures' of everyday life; family, neighbourhood, class and culture group, schooling, work and so on, and 'agency', the extent to which anyone has the ability to make key choices in their life cycle. Access to education, especially for 'late starters', especially autodidacts, can see them jump from their assumed way of life in to a separate cultural world, whose decision making choices hold greater or lesser sway in the inevitable 'snakes and ladders' of life; or as Agnes Heller (1983) put it. 'Life is an anarchy of light and shadow.' Some sociological work suggests that the 'structures' are very determining, seriously limiting the choices that people can and do make, but, a good deal of analysis argues that individuals have much more control over choices than may seem at first sight.

Throughout this essay I have made reference to 'community', and discussed culture groups as often being semi-autonomous and self-help formations in relation to particular localities and cultural lives. I have included here an article written in 2014/15, setting out some very general ideas about alternative ways of thinking about meeting the basic and everyday needs of people. I had been prompted by a familiar concern with the increasing withdrawal of the national State apparatus from long term 'welfare' commitments and the down-grading, and the deliberate drying up of funds for Local Government. I had discussed some of these key issues in my 2006 book, 'Professionalism and Practice: culture, values and service.' And also in my 2018 book on the education of professional practitioners. The big issue with this piece is of course the subsequent experience of the Covid-19 Pandemic on the UK population in terms of community support, self-help, empathy and the kindness of strangers. As has been acknowledged now the paucity of basic life support systems for localities was exposed by the various stages of the Pandemic. Despite all the debate and argument that followed the end of the Pandemic not much has changed within local communities and their culture groups. The essential cultural infrastructure is still patchy and inconsistent.

Public Service, Community Building and the role of Social Enterprise.

It is a Sociological truism that social change is constant, if uneven, and that its management will always remain a major issue for all citizens of our society. One aspect of such change is a constant focus on the inter-relation between social issues; or social problems; and personal troubles. For example, how does any individual deal with their everyday needs, and plan for the future? How do individuals, and small social groups like families, make life less precarious, and crucially, how does any 'community' both assess needs and address them? What societal and personal benchmarks exist for effectively differentiating between needs and wants, and how does any 'community' play a role in both defining these benchmarks, and taking action to achieve them?

Community is a contested concept, and like statistics can be like a musical instrument upon which any number of different tunes are played. For example, most definitions of community incorporate the influence of culture groups, which can amongst other things be based on ethnicity, nationality, social class, gender, and region. The values of such culture groups are crucial to the ways in which both the assessment of, and the response to need is made. The real life experience of diverse culture groups, like communities in general have created an extensive fund of knowledge, the know-how for coping with the 'snakes and ladders' struggles of everyday life, practical solutions to evident and often unmet need. We call this social capital, and importantly a good deal of this exists, and is a daily currency, regardless of the role of the State. So, responses to need is a vital aspect of recognition of need and appropriate responses to it. Some people, usually because of their wealth, their private capital, can enter the market place and buy what-ever 'welfare'; care, benefit, and services; they need. Most people do however rely on some collectively generated welfare provision. We usually call this 'The Welfare State'. We know that one dimension of this social phenomenon of provision for need is a recognition that self-help, individually and collectively, is often necessary. Does this mean therefore that as members of particular communities, by choice or otherwise, we are altruistic citizens? If so how altruistic are we? Do we act on the basis of enlightened self-interest? Do we believe that cooperation is both efficient and effective, and the fairest way to achieve the 'good society' by challenging disadvantage.

This discussion does inevitably raise questions about other forms of sustainability, for example the creation and maintenance of sustainable employment with sufficient incomes. Looking at the success of public sector housing over the last century confirms that without adequate and secure incomes residents will be unable to maintain a good quality of life via access to housing alone. This aspect of the social issues and personal troubles context to policy making also emphasises that any policy makers should be aware of both the intended and the unintended consequences of their actions. It is inevitable that these and other such questions are part of the moral context to our everyday lives. The quotidian is unimaginable without discussions taking place about values and the ethical basis of social life and personal considerations.

For many years now that quotidian has included understandings about the role of the State, nationally and locally, in the assessment of and response to needs. In the domains of health, care, benefits and services (like education), citizens have been assured that the State would take a lead in addressing needs for both collectives and individuals. When we talk about the Public Sector this is what we are considering. However, how often do we pause to ask ourselves what is the nature of this 'Public'? In recent years the shifts in political ideology has meant that the vanguard role of the State has been increasingly questioned. In large part this is because of the move from a Social Democratic policy making paradigm to a Neo-Liberal one. 'Big State' to 'Small State' has been the political rhetoric, while in reality the result of change in this respect has been inconsistent to say the least. The politics of selfishness has been evident, but has it worked? In some regards governments driven by Neo-Liberal ideology have actually concentrated more power in to the hands of Secretaries of State, and made policy that in fact restricted choices that citizens can make. We have for example witnessed the espousing of ideas

153

around the State still remaining the guiding hand, the impresario of meeting needs, while withdrawing from the actual frontline of funding, organisation and service delivery. One consequence of such social and political changes has been the argument that the market; the private or commercial sector, should and could play a greater efficient and effective role. However, this approach to provision often eschews universality in favour of the particular ability of users to pay at the point of need. The voluntary sector has also seen its increasing contribution promoted, and while seeking to maintain a policy and practice of universality has often been hampered by the actions of the centralised State, particularly with regard to sustained funding.

We also know that many policy initiatives are taken by ideologically driven political parties; in government or not; and that as a consequence many mistakes are made. Matthew Taylor makes this point in his article 'The Policy Presumption' (in the Royal Society of Arts (RSA) Journal no.4 2014) and also reminds us of a growing, but not new, disenchantment amongst citizens with such forms of policy making. We should always remind ourselves that while elected politicians at all levels claim they have a mandate to make and implement policy, their actual authority is regularly compromised because authority = power + legitimation, and that legitimacy has seeped away. At any one time the particular paradigm that drives policy making tends to exclude any alternative perspectives, or the consideration of alternative discourses on need and how to address it. These 'alternatives' would actually include the users of provisions.

While all these discussions and policy changes have been happening, the practitioners of many kinds who have staffed the various State organisations, have carried on delivering care and benefits and services. It has usually been the case that these people, all citizens and service users themselves of course, have been left out of policy making discussions. What local practitioners know and do remains a crucial aspect of the social capital, the know-how, of any community. It is also the case that the education and training of most practitioners has been greatly influenced by the social sciences, which has tended to emphasise the necessity to see reason as the guiding principle in both policy making and professional practice. This is essentially an aspect of professionals 'making sense of themselves', and their roles. This is particularly reflected in the critical role of theory in the research processes necessary to the understanding and analysis of need and appropriate responses. So to lose this expertise and input poses serious questions about the ability of any community to both assess and respond to need. As human beings, and maybe because of om altruism; reciprocity and empathy feature strongly on our collective moral compass? A further crucial question should be considered by all those who seek to engage in what could be broadly described as 'social working' that is, what is the nature of this 'social' with which we are seeking to work, perhaps in responding to needs?

Networks and networking are essential means to achieving desired ends. Building the capacity of any community to both assess need and respond effectively and efficiently to it is a key issue. However, there has to be a point of focus for these individual and social actions. Who is to give leadership, co-ordinate and facilitate the 'people-power' that is both latent and expressed within any community? One aspect of the liberal-democratic society in which we live has been a widely held belief that our political representatives were the essential conduits through which our values, desires and goals would be directed in order to meet those societal and individual needs. However, it is very evident that many, even most people in society today, have lost faith in the political 'class' to fulfil this key role. As discussed above ordinary people look around them and see a 'democratic deficit' at the heart of decision making and action taking. It is in part because of this current malaise that citizens have been calling for are-assessment of the role of the community" even their community, in everyday life.

One very significant aspect of these discussions about social change, need, production and provision, has been an assessment of the role of Social Enterprise. It has been argued that Social Enterprises offer a locally base more rapid response, 'can-do' attitude, a solution to both the on-going assessment of needs, and the devising of ways and means to address that. Advocates of Social Enterprises have also argued that accountability and governance stand more of chance of success in these more locally responsive approaches.

I would argue that every community, however defined should have a rapid response action research base, which can for example take referrals to address certain issues, and devise ways of addressing those issues. This would accentuate the value of the network, collaborating with a range of stakeholders who share an interest in creatively providing practical solutions to problems. Clearly the identification of potential and actual stakeholders, and an understanding of the manner of their contribution to deliberation, assessment and action, would have to be coordinated from the research base. But, the research base itself should be flexible enough to reflect the specific nature of the task under consideration. The knowledge, expertise and experience located in the diverse range of stakeholders would be reservoir to be drawn from as needed and agreed. Groups and individuals, research minded practitioners, could be 'commissioned' to contribute at some stage in the assessment and provision process.

These provisions in themselves will not be a complete solution to meeting local need because of the continuing influence of 'national' economic and political contexts. The influence of these factors may well be in a significant period of transition to other configurations, and the shifts in the discourses on need and how to respond to this, may well accelerate change elsewhere? We can certainly hope so!

John Astley 4/2015

Critical education practice

I hope that over many years of Sociological, and essentially educational, practice I have made and used theory in the pursuit and development of knowledge in order to apply this to practical solutions to meet educational needs.

I have already discussed the characteristics of Critical Practice (CP) and as theoretical and methodological approach that has kept me on a clear path of sociological practice. And, while discussing educational interventions it is worth reiterating the basic tenets of CP, which fall into three aspects. Firstly, Critical Action (as discussed above) which emphasises sound skill base used with awareness of context, operating to challenge structural disadvantage and working with difference towards empowerment. Secondly, Critical Reflexivity; an engaged self, negotiated understanding and interventions and questioning personal assumptions and values, and finally, Critical Analysis; evaluation of knowledge, theories, policies and practice, recognition of multiple perspectives, different levels of analysis e.g. up close or the long shot, and ongoing enquiry.

These three elements of CP can be viewed in any order, the point however, is that they are all in their way key components which are essential to the total; there is a dialectical process at work here.

In the design and delivery of curriculum I have shared my thinking with my students and colleagues, to make more sense of our roles and purpose. What we say, what I have said, writing and talking, is an aspect of our vocabulary of motives, drawing as it does on our values, and trying to avoid travelling down academic cul-de-sacs.

An example of this concern is my being asked in the 1990s by the University of Plymouth to design an undergraduate pathway within their

157

Humanities offer. They and I were very keen to write a course that drew on the key concerns of Cultural Studies, but, and it was a big but, that the course should be focused on the practice aspects of such a study. This aim was to prepare graduates to seek employment in the arts and cultural strategy fields, including an understanding and hands-on familiarity with developing technologies. Knowing and Doing. I have included here the frontispiece of my report.

A new academic pathway

**A report for the Faculty of Arts and Education
By John Astley   July 1997**

**BA (Hons) Cultural
Interpretation and Practice***

An innovative, exciting degree pathway which enables you to explore and develop skills, techniques and ideas important to your life and career(s) in the next millennium. It is suitable for students from a wide range of academic and other backgrounds.

Solely studying out culture (and other cultures) is not enough: practicing and training in vocational skills is not enough. But together, interpretation and practice lead to a new kind of de-gree experience at the University of Plymouth. It stems from a supportive academic environ-ment, yet is grounded in the realities of the world you enter as a successful graduate.

In conclusion

I have attempted in this essay to create a resource that readers, whoever they may be, can develop ideas, both mine, those of others cited in this text, and crucially, their own. My hope is that readers will continue to read, and discuss the issues raised in this essay, and develop ideas drawn from examples of their own experience, a grounded aesthetics in action, which takes us all from the ideal state of thoughts and conjecture to 'concrete' evidence emphasising the level of consciousness and imagination in the process. I hope that my empathy for readers, and those I write about, does manifest itself, and that what I have said about my Sociological practice in relation to my values and value orientation; what I have said and done, is clear to readers. The pursuance of the 'good society' has always been a key aim in all aspects of my practice. For example, writing for my local newspaper, and encouraging, through commissioning, other people to write is important. As I have already said it is essential to bring my Sociological skills and experience to shed light on the lives of us all by, for example encouraging people to take responsibility for their own liberation in a context of everyday life shared with others. Thinking about the lives we have, and might have, is a part of the fuel that drives an aspiration for a better life for all. Cultural Studies, the study of culture has, given its hybrid nature, opened up ways of thinking and doing that expressly take issue with the status quo of existing ideas and the material world in which we all live our everyday cultural lives.

Let me finish with William Morris writing in the mid-1850s, emphasising the demand on us all to deal with the issues which confront us;

'In spite of all the success I have had, I have not failed to be conscious that the art I have been helping to produce would fall with the death of a few of us who really care about it…Both my historical studies and my practical conflict with the philistinism of modern society have forced on me the conviction that art cannot have a real life and growth under the present system of

159

commercialism and profit-mongering. I have tried to develop this view, which is in fact Socialism seen through the eyes of an artist...'

Index

Davies, William, 5
democracy, 8, 9, 12, 54, 64, 65, 68,
    72, 104, 105
Eagleton, Terry, 4, 6, 17, 24, 25,
    27, 50, 56, 108
economic, 4, 7, 9, 12, 18, 19, 21,
    28, 30, 31, 40, 43, 45, 46, 47,
    61, 86, 94, 97, 103, 106, 108,
    113
education, 1, 2, 5, 11, 12, 23, 24,
    31, 34, 36, 39, 59, 63, 65, 72,
    78, 81, 84, 88, 90, 92, 95, 98,
    104, 105, 109, 110, 111, 113
Empire, 22, 70
Erickson, Frederick, 76
everyday life, 3, 4, 6, 7, 8, 10, 12,
    14, 16, 20, 23, 26, 29, 30, 31,
    34, 35, 36, 37, 39, 40, 43, 47,
    49, 52, 53, 56, 59, 60, 70, 71,
    76, 77, 78, 86, 89, 91, 94, 98,
    101, 102, 103, 107, 108, 109,
    110, 112, 114
Exmouth Journal, 73, 93, 97, 100
folk, 13, 24, 37, 41, 47, 54, 66, 67,
    69, 72
Fraser, Nancy and Jaeggi, Rahel,
    13
Freud, 38, 59, 90
Frith, Simon, 36
Gaskill, Malcolm, 8
Gilroy, Paul, 70
Goffman, 75, 77, 79, 80, 81, 82,
    83, 84, 90

Hall, 7, 14
Hall, Stuart, 29, 31, 52, 61, 70
Hegemonism, 61
hegemony, 12, 31, 48, 60, 61, 62
Heritage industry, 18
Hobsbawm, Eric, 59, 71
Hoggart, Richard, 7, 14, 19, 20,
    28, 29, 30, 31, 35, 37, 39, 41,
    51, 52, 53, 55, 56, 90, 107
ideas, 2, 3, 4, 5, 9, 14, 15, 16, 17,
    18, 20, 23, 27, 28, 31, 32, 34,
    38, 44, 48, 51, 53, 59, 60, 61,
    62, 65, 68, 71, 72, 75, 76, 77,
    80, 84, 89, 95, 96, 99, 100, 101,
    102, 107, 108, 109, 111, 114
ideology, 31, 34, 43, 45, 48, 49, 50,
    60, 61, 65, 70, 110
Johnson, Richard, 5
Kinnock, Neil, 64
knowledge, 2, 4, 5, 7, 16, 26, 34,
    37, 60, 61, 76, 80, 81, 82, 85,
    91, 92, 94, 104, 105, 107, 110,
    112, 113
Labour Party, 64
Laikola, Hanna, 33
lecture, 76, 81, 82, 83, 84
legitimacy, 54, 60, 111
Lenin, 62
Liberalism, 25
Lloyd, A L, 66
Macey, David, 16
Maglaque, Erin, 23
Mandelson, Peter, 65